Table Of Contents

THE QUILTS ● 2
Amish Beehive ● 4
Faithful Circle ● 9
Little Hexagon Spinner ● 13
Stacking Tumblers ● 16
Candy Apple Cores ● 19
Sugarloaf Mountain ● 22
Stars in the Night ● 25
Mini Dresden Flowers ● 29
Just Crazy ● 33
Hexagon Beauty ● 36
Perennial Posies ● 39

ENGLISH PAPER PIECING ● 42

MEASURING PAPER PIECES ● 42

CUTTING FABRIC ● 42

BASTING ● 44

BASTING CURVES ● 45

WHIP STITCHING ● 47

REMOVING THE PAPER PIECES ● 49

APPLIQUÉ ● 50

ADDING BORDERS ● 50

BIAS TAPE ● 52

BINDING ● 52

PORTABLE PROJECT STRATEGIES ● 53

FINISHING TOUCHES ● 54

RESOURCES ● 55

OUR FAVORITE NOTIONS ● 55

LECTURES AND WORKSHOPS ● 56

The Quilts

Amish Beehive
p. 4

Faithful Circle
p. 9

Little Hexagon Spinner
p. 13

Stacking Tumblers
p. 16

Candy Apple Cores
p. 19

Sugarloaf Mountain
p. 22

The Quilts

Stars In The Night
p. 25

Mini Dresden
Flowers
p. 29

Just Crazy
p. 33

Hexagon
Beauty
p. 36

Perennial
Posies
p. 39

Amish Beehive

By Chris Moline

Here's a different look for those honeycomb pieces - a radiating star in graduating colors! The Cherrywood fabrics are so easy to work with and they give the quilt the look of an Amish wool quilt.

Amish Beehive was quilted by Chris Moline with Bottom Line and King Tut threads. The batting used was Pellon Cotton.

Amish Beehive

Piecing Pointers – Read all instructions before beginning

Miniature Wall Hanging

Quilt Size   17" x 17"

Paper Pieces Required

168 - 1/2" Honeycombs (HON050)

Fabric Required

Pieces	Assorted Scraps: Each round uses a different color, 12 in all with the largest piece measuring 6" by 12"
Background	1/2 yard
Border	1/4 yard
Backing	20" x 20"
Batting	20" x 20"
Binding	1/8 yard

Piecing Pointers – If you are working on pieces less than an inch per side, you can travel the thread along the seam allowance and start whipping at a new point.

Cutting Instructions

Pieces   ***Note:** A strip is considered the width of the fabric from selvage to selvage.*

(168) 1-1/4" x 1-3/4" rectangles for the following:

- 4 – Light Yellow
- 4 – Gold
- 8 – Orange
- 8 – Rust
- 12 – Pink
- 12 – Red
- 16 – Lavender
- 16 – Purple
- 20 – Light Blue
- 20 – Dark blue
- 24 – Light Green
- 24 – Dark Green

Background	Cut a 16" x 16" square.
Border	Cut (2) 2-1/2" strips.
Binding	Cut (2) 1-3/4" strips.

5

Assembly Instructions

1) Baste the fabric to the Paper Pieces according to the basic instructions.

2) Sew the four Light Yellow into a cross (Fig. 1), then sew the four Gold pieces into the corners to make the center. (Fig.2)

Fig. 1 **Fig. 2**

3) Sew the following colors into the following rows.

Orange and Rust
Row A:
Make 8

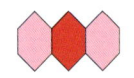

Pink, Red, and Pink
Row B:
Make 4

Red, Pink, and Red
Row C:
Make 4

Lavender, Purple, Lavender, and Purple
Row D:
Make 8

Light Blue, Dark Blue, Light Blue, Dark Blue and Light Blue
Row E:
Make 4

Dark Blue, Light Blue, Dark Blue, Light Blue, and Dark Blue
Row F:
Make 4

Light Green, Dark Green, Light Green, Dark Green Light Green, and Dark Green
Row G:
Make 8

4) Sew each Row A from the previous step to Fig. 2, starting with the rows that go on the sides and then adding the rows to the corners. (Fig. 3) ***Be careful to watch the fabric placement to be sure they alternate correctly.***

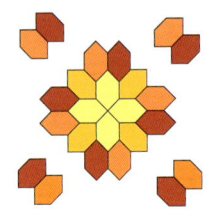

Fig. 3

5) Sew each Row B to the sides of the completed Fig.3. Sew Row C to the corners. (Fig. 4)

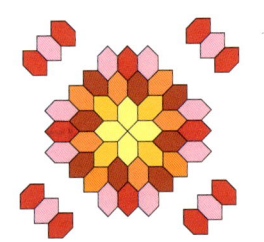

Fig. 4

6

Assembly Instructions Continued

6) Sew each Row D to Fig. 4, starting with the rows that go on the sides and then adding the rows to the corners. (Fig. 5) ***Be careful to watch the fabric placement to be sure they alternate correctly.***

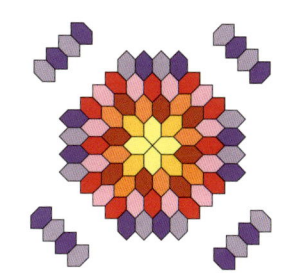

Fig. 5

7) Sew each Row E to the middles of the completed Fig. 5. Sew Row F to the corners. (Fig. 6)

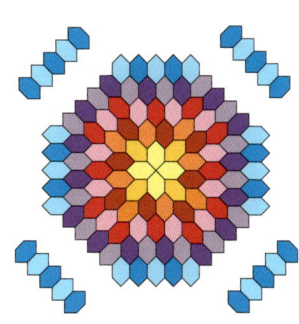

Fig. 6

8) Sew each Row G to Fig. 6, starting with the rows that go on the sides and then adding the rows to the corners. (Fig. 7) ***Be careful to watch the fabric placement to be sure they alternate correctly.***

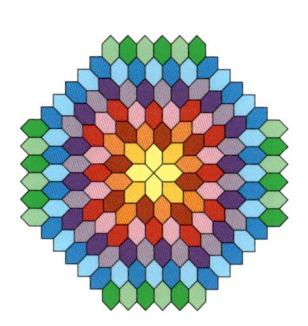

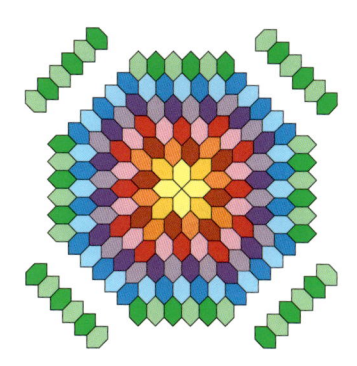

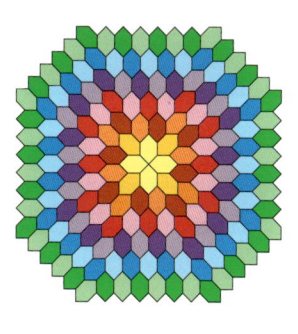

Fig. 7

9) Center and appliqué Fig. 7 to the background. See instructions on page 50. Square off background to 13-1/4" square.

Quilt Diagram

10) Remove papers. See instructions on page 50.

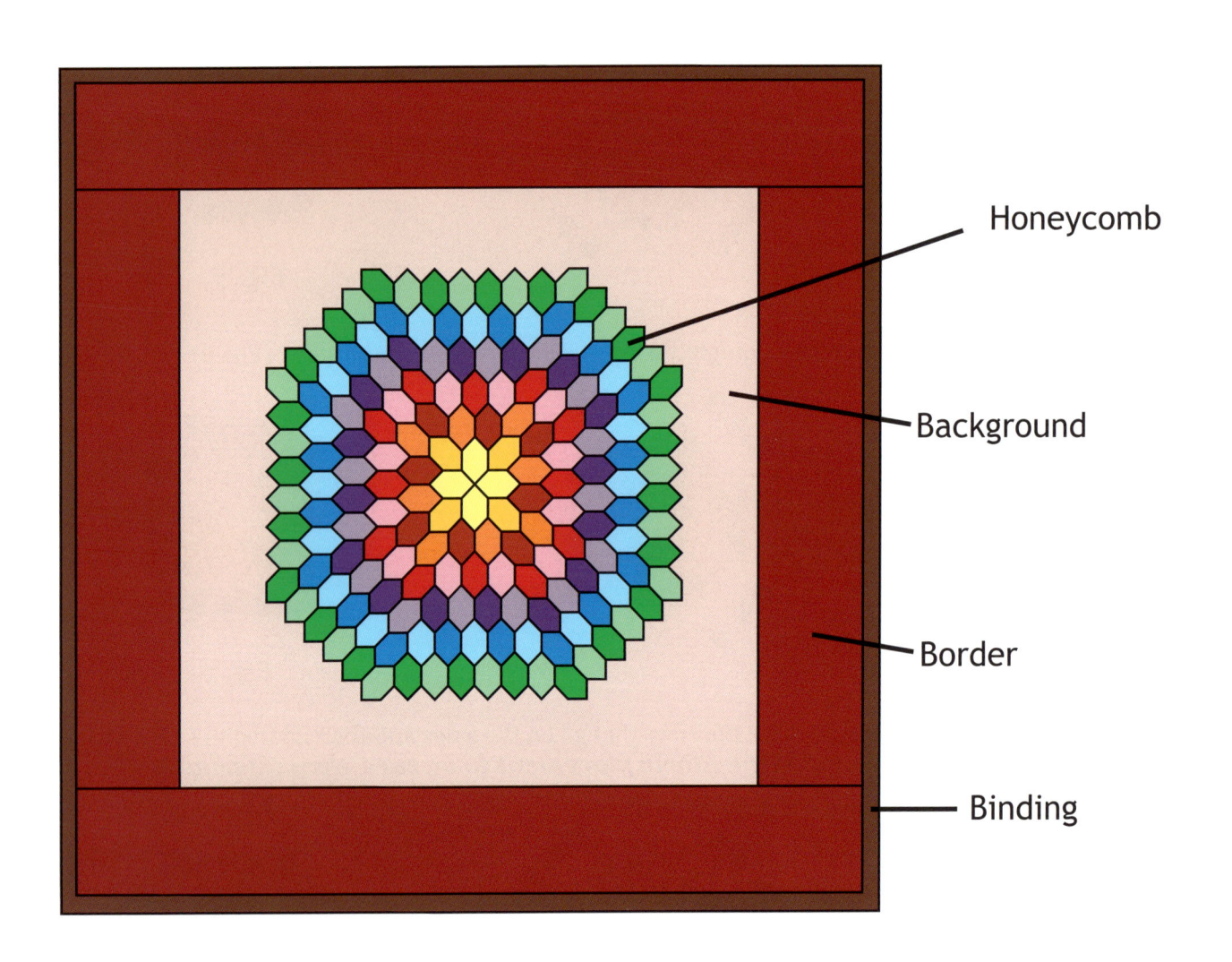

- Honeycomb
- Background
- Border
- Binding

Borders

Sew the borders to the quilt top. See instructions on page 50.

Quilting Recommendations

Amish Beehive was quilted using a continuous line design of oak leaves for the center with additional leaf motifs in the background. It was completed with a rail fence pattern in the outer borders.

Binding

Follow the instructions on page 52 for the French Fold method.

8

Faithful Circle

By Chris Moline

A nod to the Downers Grove Illinois Quilt Guild on this one – it is the symbol for the guild and a personal favorite block.

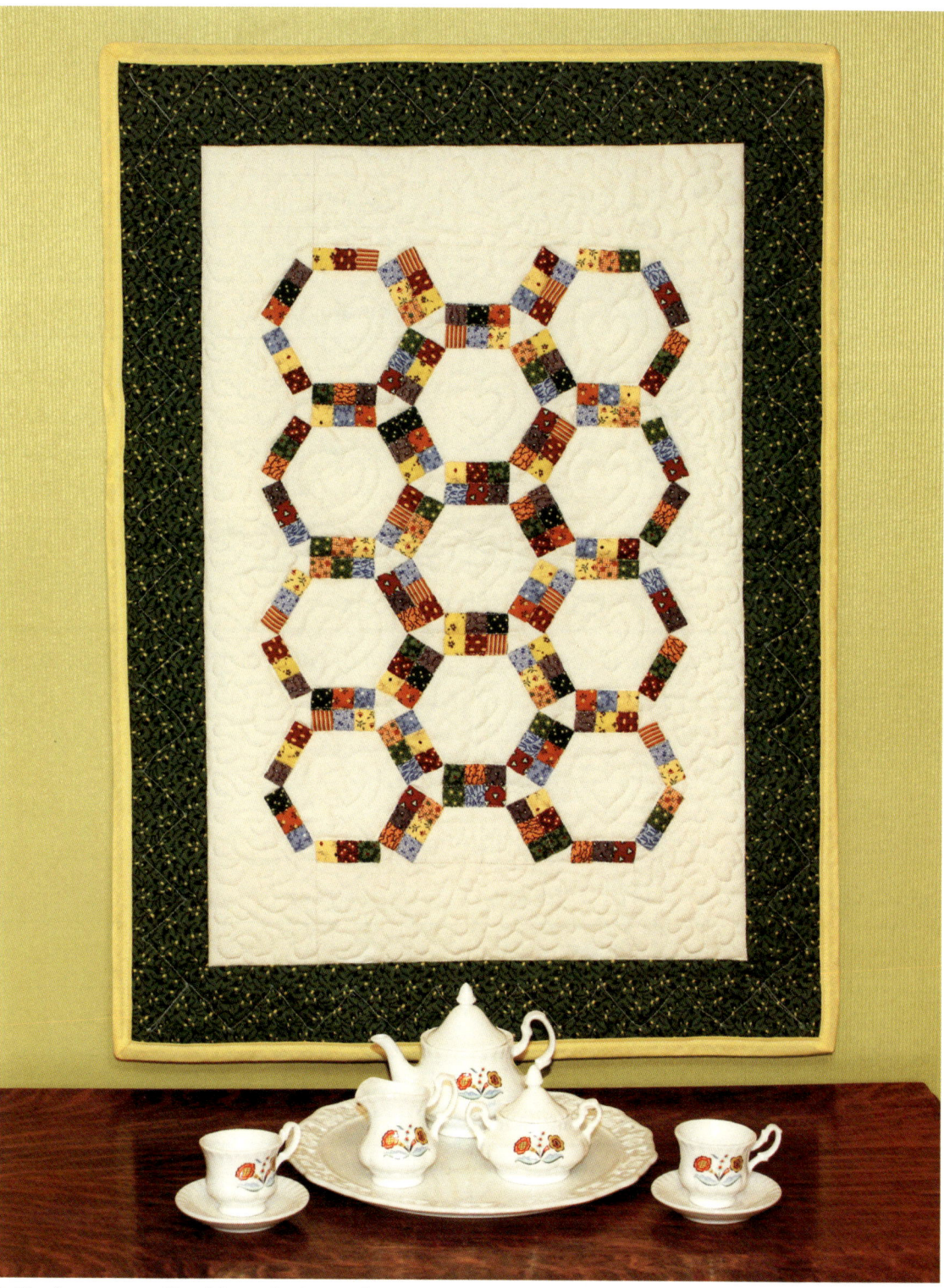

Faithful Circle was quilted by Chris Moline with Superior Threads. The batting used was Mountain Mist Cotton.

Faithful Circle

Piecing Pointers - Read all instructions before beginning

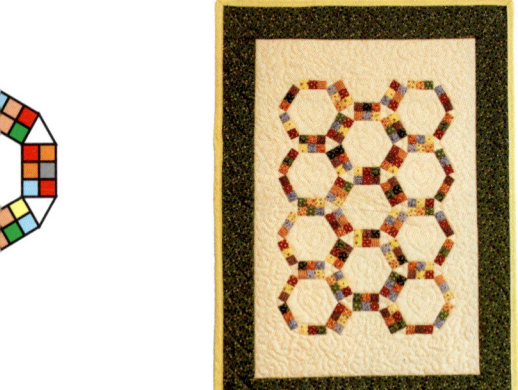

Miniature Wall Hanging

Quilt Size   17-1/2" x 23-1/2"

Paper Pieces Required

11 - 1-1/2" Hexagons (HEX150)
2 - 1-1/2" Half Hexagons (HHX150)
226 - 1/2" Squares (SQU050)
14 - 1" Triangles (TRI100)
12 - 1/2" Triangles (TRI050)
10 - 1/2" Half Hexagons (HHX050)

Fabric Required

Pieces	Assorted Print Scraps: 1/4 yard OR (18) 5" charm squares
Background and White Pieces	2/3 yard
Border	1/4 yard
Backing	20-1/2" x 26-1/2"
Batting	20-1/2" x 26-1/2"
Binding	1/8 yard

Piecing Pointers - When working with very small pieces it helps to have more than a quarter inch seam allowance. After the top is completed, you can trim the excess fabric from the back before you take out the pieces.

Cutting Instructions

Pieces   ****Note:** *A strip is considered the width of the fabric from selvage to selvage.*

Assorted Print Scraps: Cut (226) 1" squares for 1/2" squares.
White: Cut (11) 3-1/2" squares for 1-1/2" hexagons.
   Cut (2) 2" x 3" rectangles for 1-1/2" half hexagons.
   Cut (14) 1-1/2" triangles for 1" triangles.
   Cut (12) 1" triangles for 1/2" triangles.
   Cut (10) 1" x 1-1/2" rectangles for 1/2" half hexagons.

Background   Cut a 13-1/2" x 19-1/2" rectangle.

Border   Cut (2) 2-1/2" strips.

Binding   Cut (2) 1-3/4" strips.

Assembly Instructions

1) Baste the fabric to the Paper Pieces according to the basic instructions.

2) Sew 1/2" squares together into rows of 3 squares. (Fig. 1)

Fig. 1
Make 72

Assembly Instructions Continued

3) Sew 42 of the 3 square rows together. (Fig. 2)

Fig. 2
Make 21

4) Sew pieces together to form the following rows: (Fig. 3 and Fig. 4)

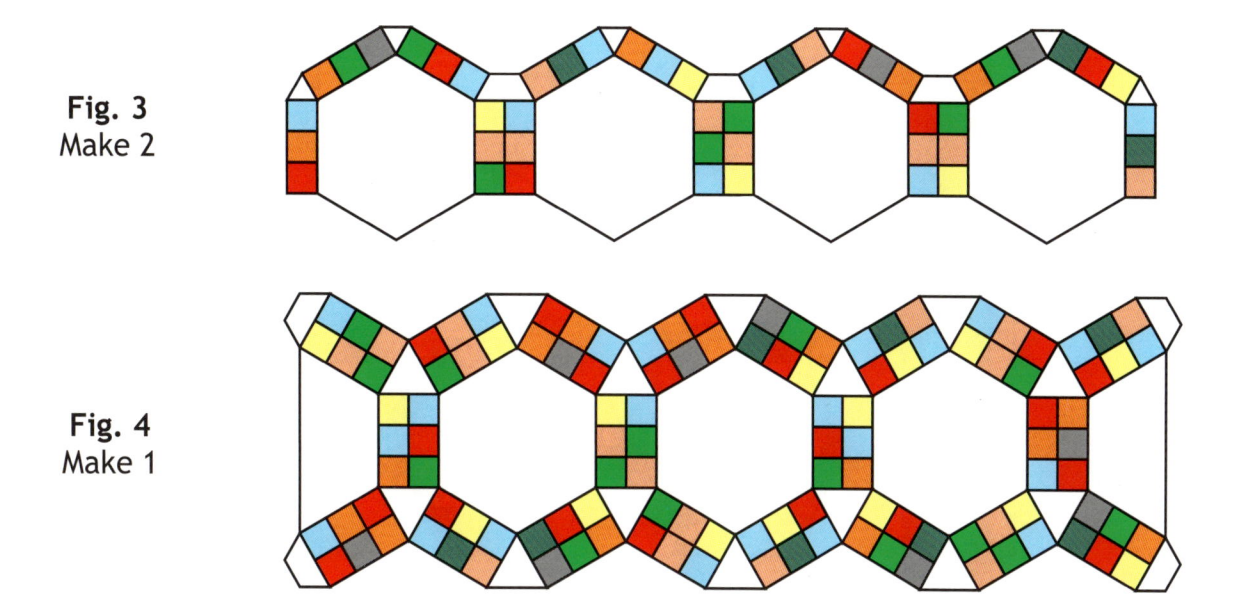

Fig. 3
Make 2

Fig. 4
Make 1

5) Sew rows together to form the completed top. (Fig. 5)

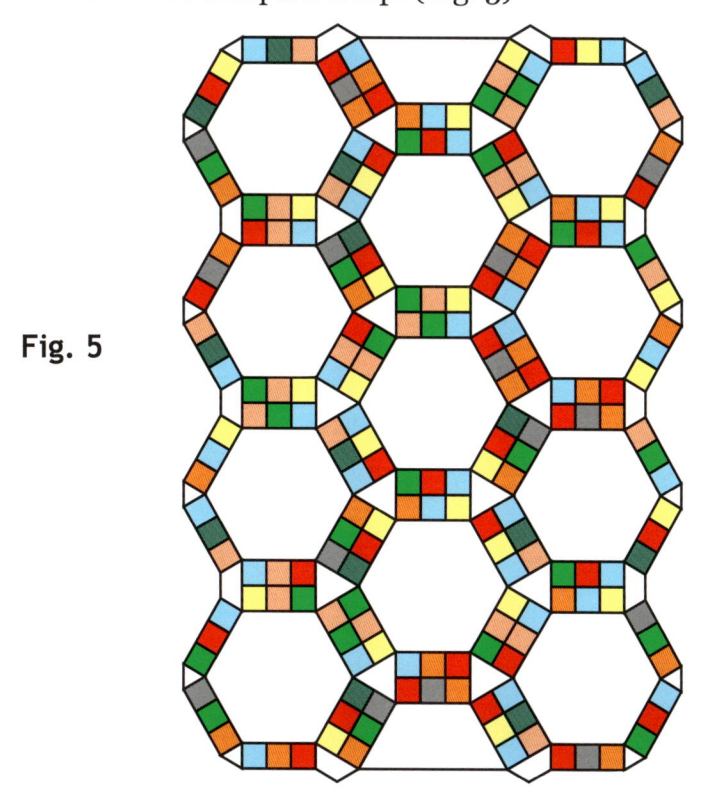

Fig. 5

11

Assembly Instructions Continued

6) Appliqué the rows to the background fabric. See instructions on page 50.

7) Remove papers. See instructions on page 50.

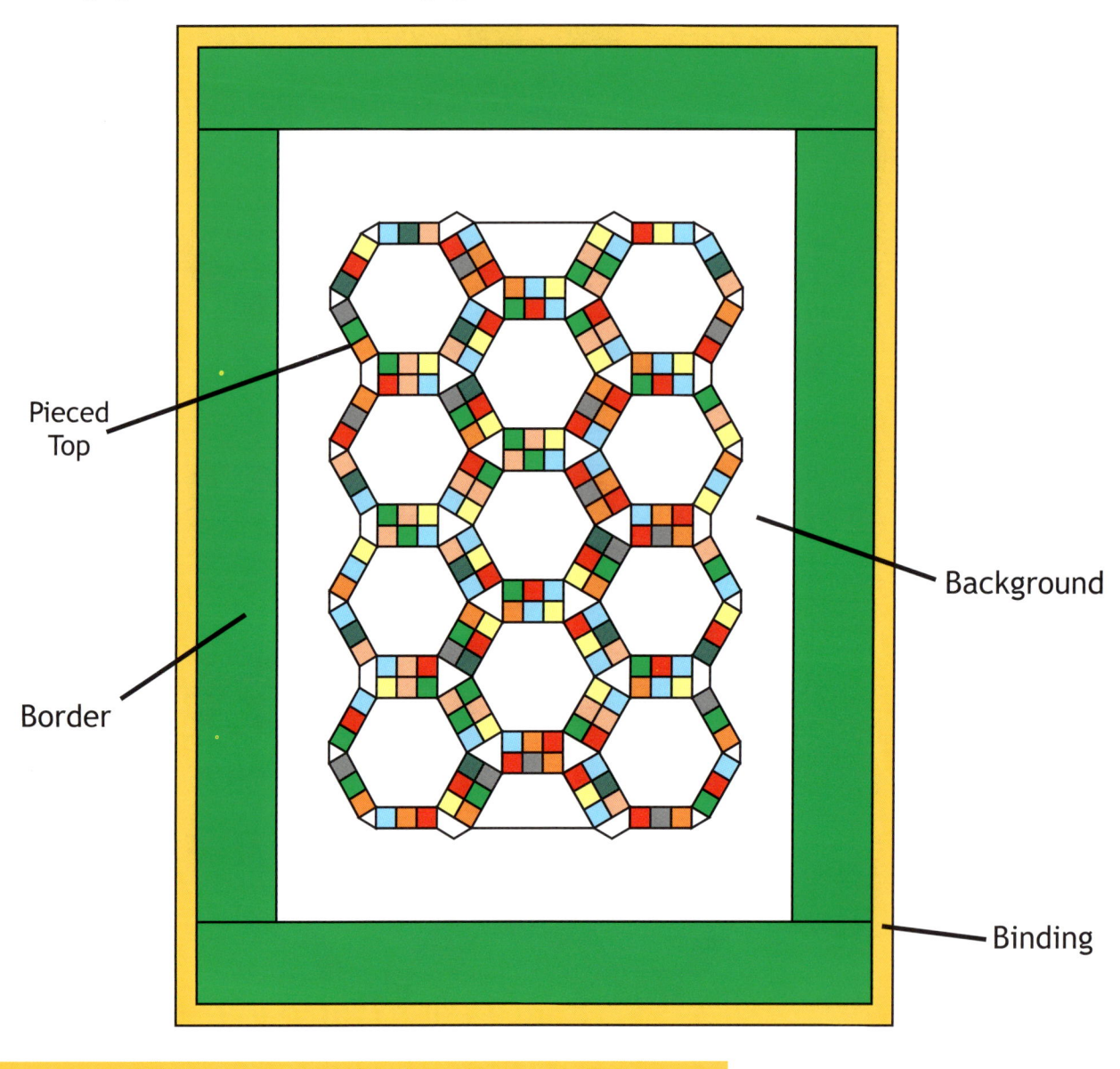

Pieced Top

Background

Border

Binding

Borders

Sew the borders to the quilt top. See instructions on page 50.

Quilting Recommendations

Faithful Circle was quilted with concentric hearts in the hexagons and then stitched in the ditch around them. The outer background was quilted with a meandering stipple and the border was done in a crosshatch.

Binding

Follow the instructions on page 52 for the French Fold method.

Little Hexagon Spinner

By JoAnne Louis

Let a splash of color spin out into your room with this miniature quilt! It's playful colors will brighten up any room.

Little Hexagon Spinner was quilted by JoAnne Louis. The batting used was Hobbs Heirloom.

Little Hexagon Spinner

Piecing Pointers - Read all instructions before beginning

Miniature Wall Hanging

Quilt Size 14-1/2" x 20"

Fabric Required

Pieces	Assorted Color Scraps: 3/8 yard total
	Black: 1/2 yard
Backing	17-1/2" x 23"
Batting	17-1/2" x 23"

Paper Pieces Required

653 - 3/8" Hexagons (HEX038)

Cutting Instructions

Pieces   ****Note:** *A strip is considered the width of the fabric from selvage to selvage.*

If cutting from strips:
Cut (10) 1-1/4" strips and then sub cut into (305) 1-1/4" squares for the Colored Hexagons.
Cut (11) 1-1/4" strips and then sub cut into (348) 1-1/4" squares for the Black Hexagons.

If piecing out your stash:
Cut (6) 1-1/4" x 1-1/4" squares of EACH color for the 32 sets of hexagons. (Fig.1)
Cut (113) 1-1/4" x 1-1/4" squares of assorted colors for the border hexagons. (Fig. 3)

Assembly Instructions

1) Baste the fabric to the Paper Pieces according to the basic instructions.

2) Sew six colored pieces together to form a triangle. (Fig.1)

Fig. 1
Make 32

3) Sew together the following rows.

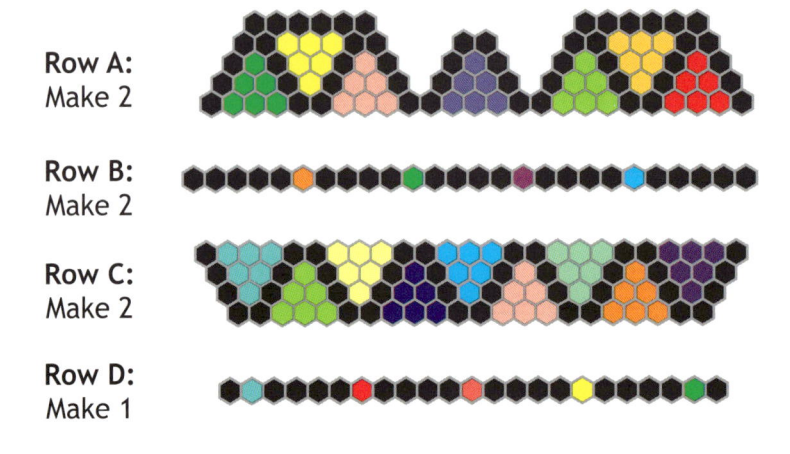

Row A: Make 2

Row B: Make 2

Row C: Make 2

Row D: Make 1

Assembly Instructions Continued

4) Sew the rows together in the following order. (Fig.2)

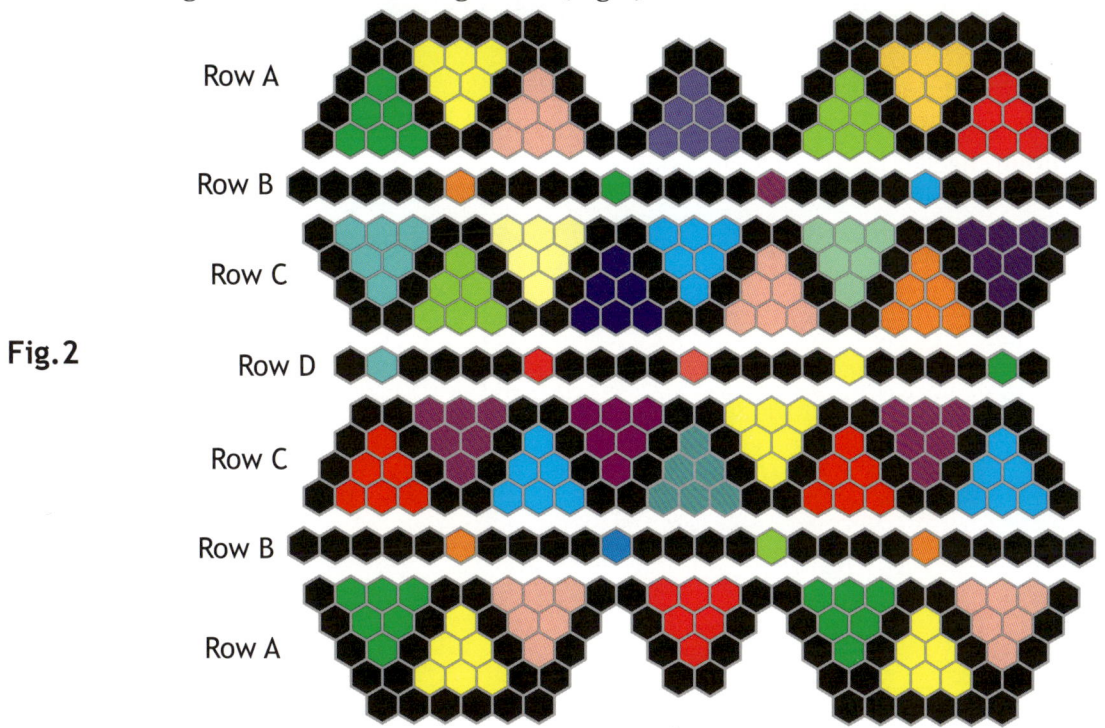

Fig. 2

Row A
Row B
Row C
Row D
Row C
Row B
Row A

5) Sew the remaining colored hexagons around the perimeter. Then sew the remaining black hexagons around the perimeter. (Fig.3)

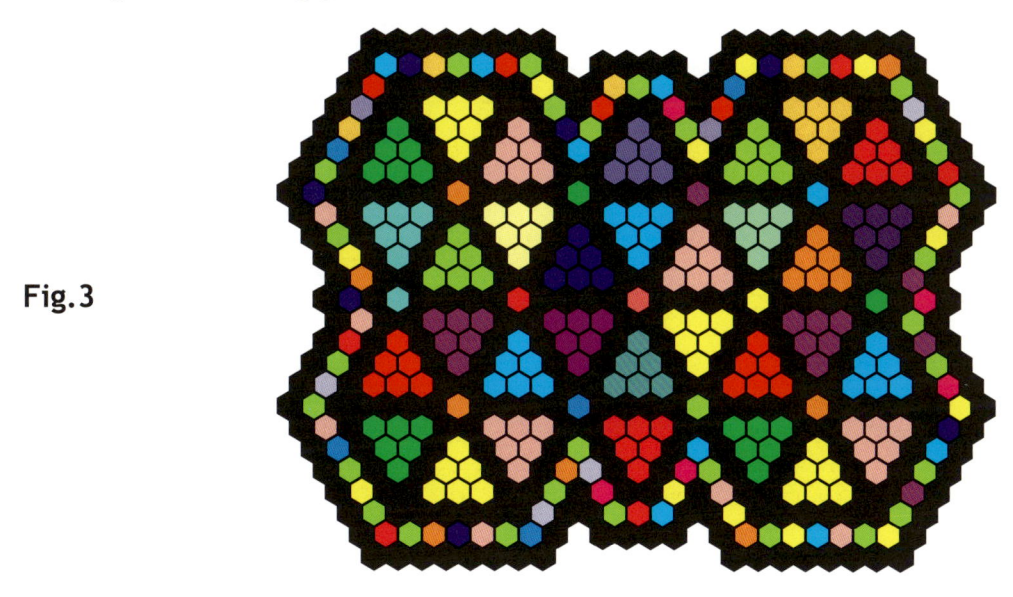

Fig. 3

6) Remove papers. See instructions on page 49.

Quilting Recommendations

Little Hexagon Spinner was quilted with a small loop design in the black hexagons to make the colored areas stand out.

Finishing

Follow the instructions on page 52 for the Knife Edge method.

15

Stacking Tumblers

By JoAnne Louis

This charming quilt was a great way to piece out our 1930's prints collection. Alternating it with a classic white creates a unique checker board affect in a modern way.

Stacking Tumblers was quilted by Chris Moline with Superior Threads. The batting used was Pellon's Legacy.

Stacking Tumblers

Piecing Pointers - Read all instructions before beginning

Miniature Wall Hanging

| Quilt Size | 20-1/2" x 24" |

Paper Pieces Required

361 - 1" Tumblers (TUM100)

Fabric Required

Pieces	Assorted Print Scraps: 1/2 yard
	White: 1/2 yard
Background	2/3 yard
Backing	23-1/2" x 27"
Batting	23-1/2" x 27"
Binding	1/4 yard
Rickrack	3 yards

Piecing Pointers - Let the focus be on your quilt and not your stitches. Always take the time to match your threads to the darker colors of your fabrics.

Cutting Instructions

Pieces   ****Note:** *A strip is considered the width of the fabric from selvage to selvage.*

If cutting from strips:
Cut (9) 1-3/4" strips and then sub cut into (180) 1-3/4" x 1-3/4" squares for the print tumblers.
Cut (9) 1-3/4" strips and then sub cut into (181) 1-3/4" x 1-3/4" squares for the white tumblers.

If piecing out your stash:
Cut (180) 1-3/4" x 1-3/4" squares of assorted colors for the print tumblers.

Background   Cut a 20-1/2" x 24" rectangle.

Binding   Cut (3) 2-1/2" strips.

Assembly Instructions

1) Baste the fabric to the Paper Pieces according to the basic instructions.

2) Alternating white and print tumbler pieces, whip stitch the tumblers into the following rows:

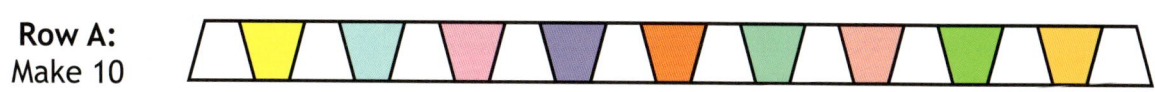

Row A: Make 10

Row B: Make 9

Assembly Instructions Continued

3) Starting at the top, whip stitch all of the rows together making sure to alternate between Row A and Row B. (Fig.1) There should be a total of 19 rows starting and ending with Row A.

Fig.1

4) Center and appliqué completed top to the background. See instructions on page 50. Square off to 19-1/2" x 23".

5) Remove papers. See instructions on page 50.

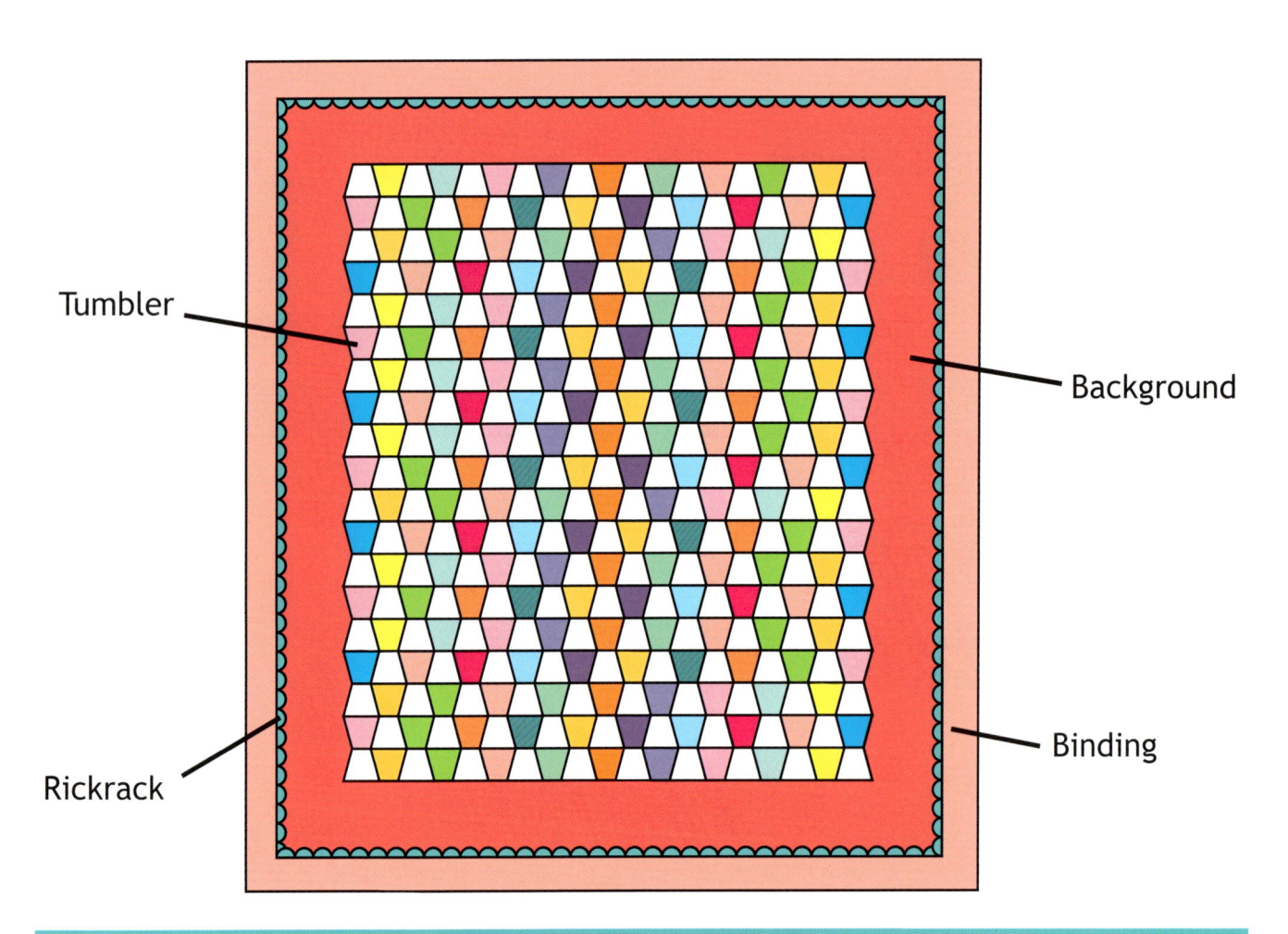

Tumbler

Background

Rickrack

Binding

Quilting Recommendations

Stacking Tumblers was quilted with a loop in each white tumbler and then echo quilted in the borders.

Binding

Follow the instructions on page 52 for the rickrack binding.

18

Candy Apple Cores

By Chris Moline

These bite sized treats are a wonder once they are completed and put together. Using a cream colored background draws your eyes to the real treats that make up this quilt - the miniature apple cores!

Candy Apple Cores was quilted by Chris Moline with Superior Threads. The batting used was Pellon's Legacy.

Candy Apple Cores

Piecing Pointers - Read all instructions before beginning

Miniature Wall Hanging

Quilt Size 17" x 17-3/4"

Paper Pieces Required

380 - 1" Apple Core (APP1)

Fabric Required

Pieces	Assorted scraps 5/8 yard
Background	1/2 yard
Backing	20" x 20-3/4"
Batting	20" x 20-3/4"
Binding	1/4 yard

Piecing Pointers - Have fun with the arrangement! Go totally random, alternate light and dark fabrics, or create a custom design.

Cutting Instructions

Pieces   **Note:** A strip is considered the width of the fabric from selvage to selvage.

If cutting from strips:
Cut (13) 1-1/2" strips and then sub cut into (380) 1-1/4" x 1-1/2" rectangles for the apple cores.

If piecing out your stash:
Cut (380) 1-1/4" x 1-1/2" rectangles of assorted colors for the apple cores.

Background   Cut an 18" x 18-3/4" rectangle.

Binding   Cut (3) 1-3/4" strips.

Assembly Instructions

1) Baste the fabric to the Paper Pieces according to the curved basting instructions on page 45.

2) Whip stitch the apple cores into rows using the whip stitching curves instructions on page 48. (Fig.1)

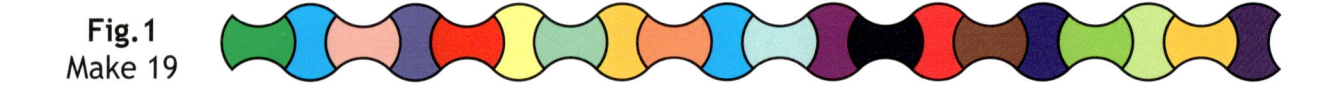

Fig. 1
Make 19

Assembly Instructions Continued

3) Whip stitch the rows in Fig.1 together to complete the center. (Fig.2)

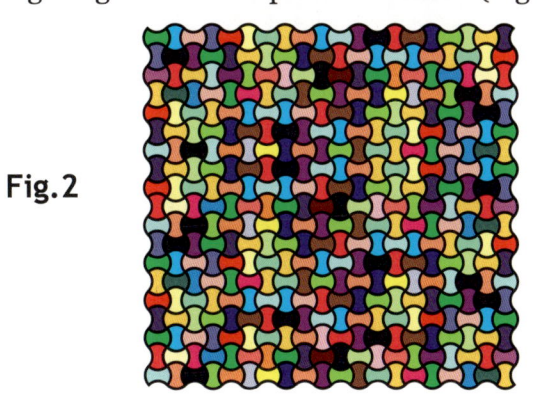

Fig. 2

4) Appliqué center to background. See instructions on page 50.

5) Remove papers. See instructions on page 50.

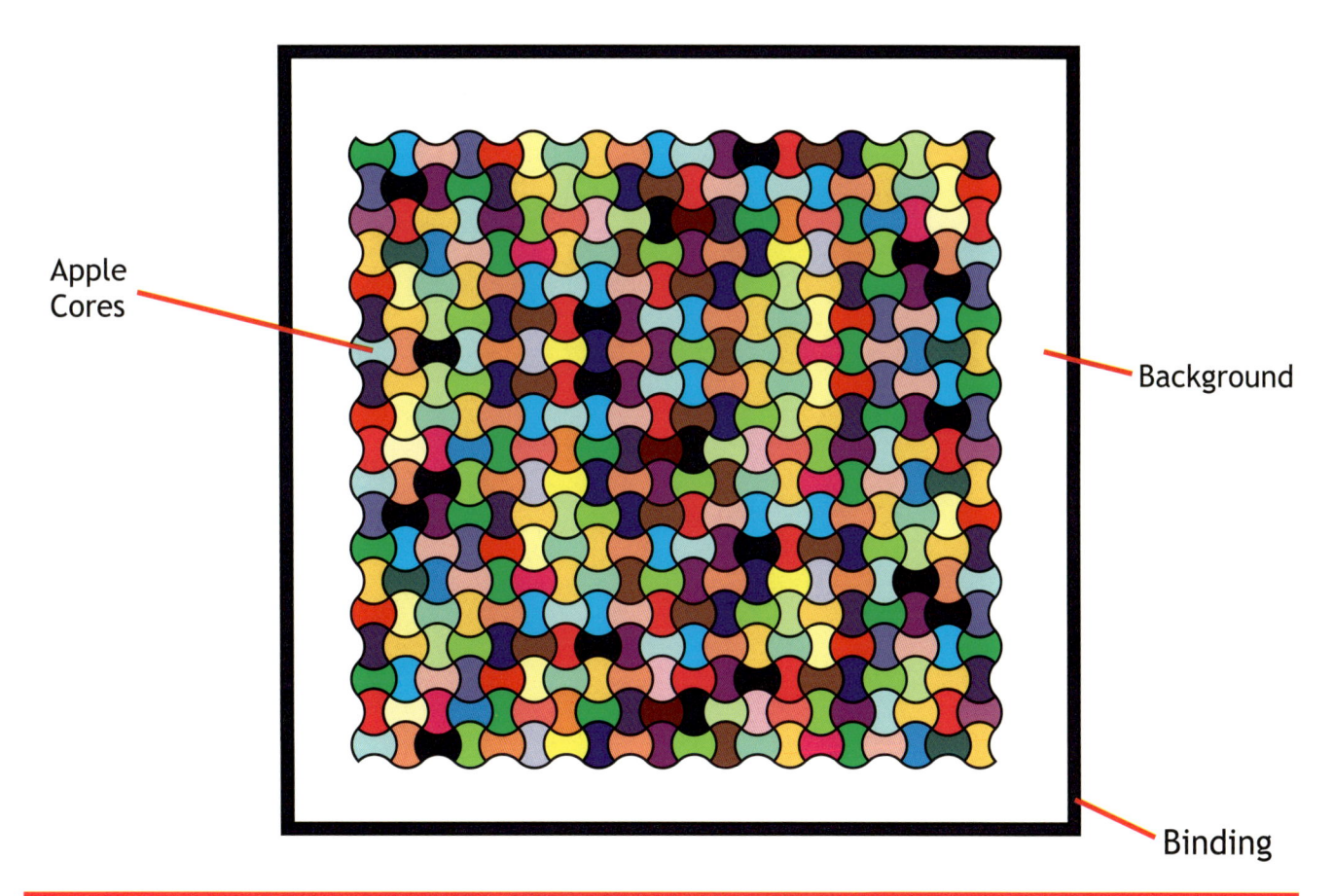

Apple Cores

Background

Binding

Quilting Recommendations

Candy Apple Cores was quilted in the ditch for the center of the quilt. The borders were echo quilted for a few rows and then stippled.

Binding

Follow the instructions on page 52 for the French Fold method.

Sugarloaf Mountain

By Chris Moline

Sugarloaf Mountain is a creation in Civil War scrap fabrics. All the peaks and valleys are so easy with Paper Piecing it makes this quilt a quick and rewarding project!

Sugarloaf Mountain was quilted by Chris Moline with Gutermann Quilting thread. Batting used was Hobbs Wool.

Sugarloaf Mountain

Piecing Pointers - Read all instructions before beginning

Fabric Required

Pieces	Off-White*: 1/2 yard Prints: *1/2 yard of assorted scraps see details below*
Border*	1/8 yard
Backing*	20" x 24"
Batting	20" x 24"
Binding	1/8 yard

*Same Fabric

Wall Hanging
Quilt Size   16" x 18-1/2"

Paper Pieces Required
168 - 2" x 1-1/4" Triangles (ITRI200)

Piecing Pointers - To maintain the sharp points of the triangles, be sure to let the tails wag. The tail will lay flat behind the next piece after they are whipped together.

Cutting Instructions

Pieces ****Note** a strip is considered the width of the fabric from selvage to selvage.

If cutting from strips:
   Cut (9) 2" strips and then sub cut into (88) 2" x 3" rectangles for the off-white triangles.
   Cut (9) 2" strips and then sub cut into (80) 2" x 3" rectangles for the print triangles.

If piecing out your stash:
   Cut (80) 2" x 3" rectangles of assorted colors for the print triangles.

Border	Cut (2) 2" strips.
Binding	Cut (2) 1-3/4" strips.

Assembly Instructions

1) Baste the fabric to the Paper Pieces according to the basic instructions.

2) Alternating pieces, whipstitch 10 print and 11 off white triangles into a straight row. (Fig.1)

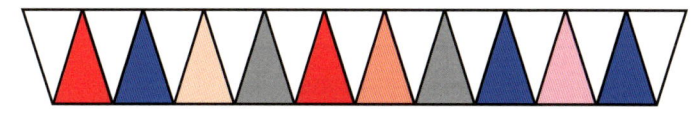

Fig.1
Make 8 Rows

23

Assembly Instructions Continued

3) Starting at the top, whipstitch all of the rows together. Make sure to match the points of one row with the centers of the next row. (Fig.2)

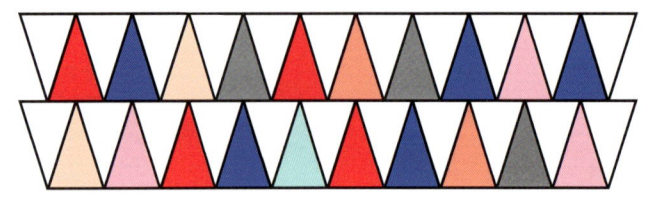

Fig. 2

4) Remove papers. See instructions on page 49.

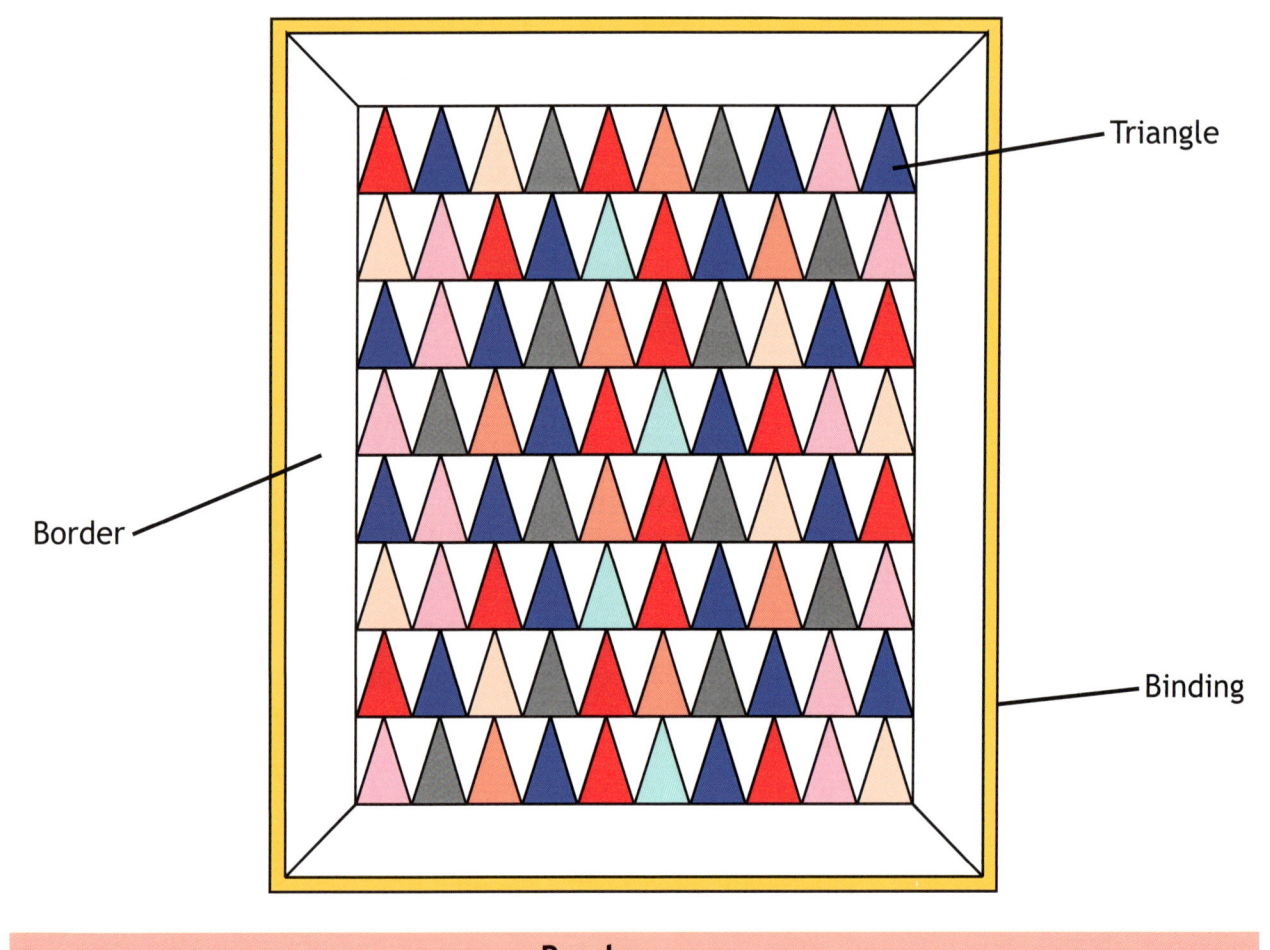

Triangle

Border

Binding

Borders

Sew the borders to the quilt top using mitered corners. See instructions on pages 50 and 51.

Quilting Recommendations

Sugarloaf Mountain was quilted with ditch quilting to make the mountains stand out. An overall design would also work well.

Binding

Follow the instructions on page 52 for the French Fold method.

Stars In The Night

By JoAnne Louis

The dazzling colors of the fabric are dramatically set apart from the dark background fabric just like stars on a clear night.

Stars In The Night was quilted by Basket Cases in Clare, Illinois.

25

Stars In The Night

Piecing Pointers - Read all instructions before beginning

Miniature Wall Hanging

Quilt Size   23" x 24-3/4"

Paper Pieces Required

145 - 1" 6 Point/60 Degree Diamonds (6DIA100)

Fabric Required

Pieces	Assorted Color Scraps: 1/4 yard
	Black: 1/2 yard*
Background*	1/2 yard
Inner Border	Assorted Color Scraps: 1/8 yard
Outer Border*	1/2 yard
Backing	26" x 27-3/4"
Batting	26" x 27-3/4"
Binding	1/4 yard

*Same fabric

Cutting Instructions

Pieces   ****Note:** *A strip is considered the width of the fabric from selvage to selvage.*

If cutting from strips:
     Cut (6) 1-1/2" strips and then sub cut into (108) 60 degree diamonds for colored diamonds.
     Cut (2) 1-1/2" strips and then sub cut into (37) 60 degree diamonds for black diamonds.

If piecing out your stash:
     Cut (6) 1-1/2" 60 degree diamonds of EACH color for the 18 sets of stars. (Fig.1)

Background   Cut a 16-1/4" x 18" rectangle.

Inner Border   Cut (52) 1-1/2" x 2" rectangles.

Outer Border   Cut (3) 3-1/2" strips.

Binding   Cut (3) 2-1/2" strips.

Assembly Instructions

1) Baste the fabric to the Paper Pieces according to the basic instructions.

2) Sew six 60 degree diamonds together to form stars. (Fig.1)

Fig.1
Make 18

26

Assembly Instructions Continued

3) Add the black diamonds to the stars in Fig.1 to create the following rows.

Row A: Make 2

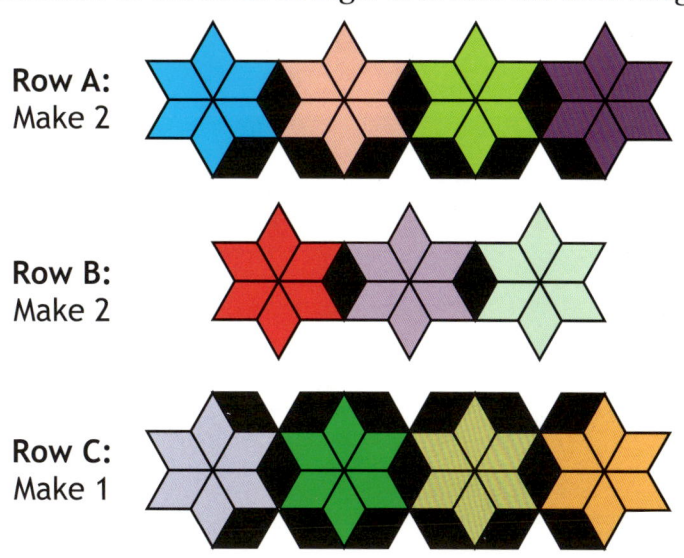

Row B: Make 2

Row C: Make 1

4) Sew the rows together in the following order. (Fig.2)

Fig. 2

Row A

Row B

Row C

Row B

Row A

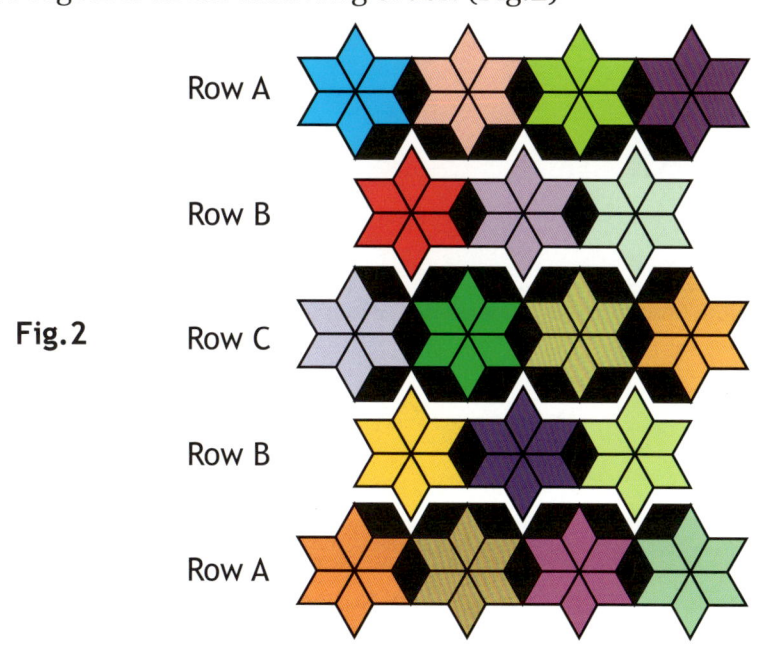

5) Appliqué to background. See instructions on page 50.

27

Assembly Instructions Continued

6) Remove papers. See instructions on page 50.

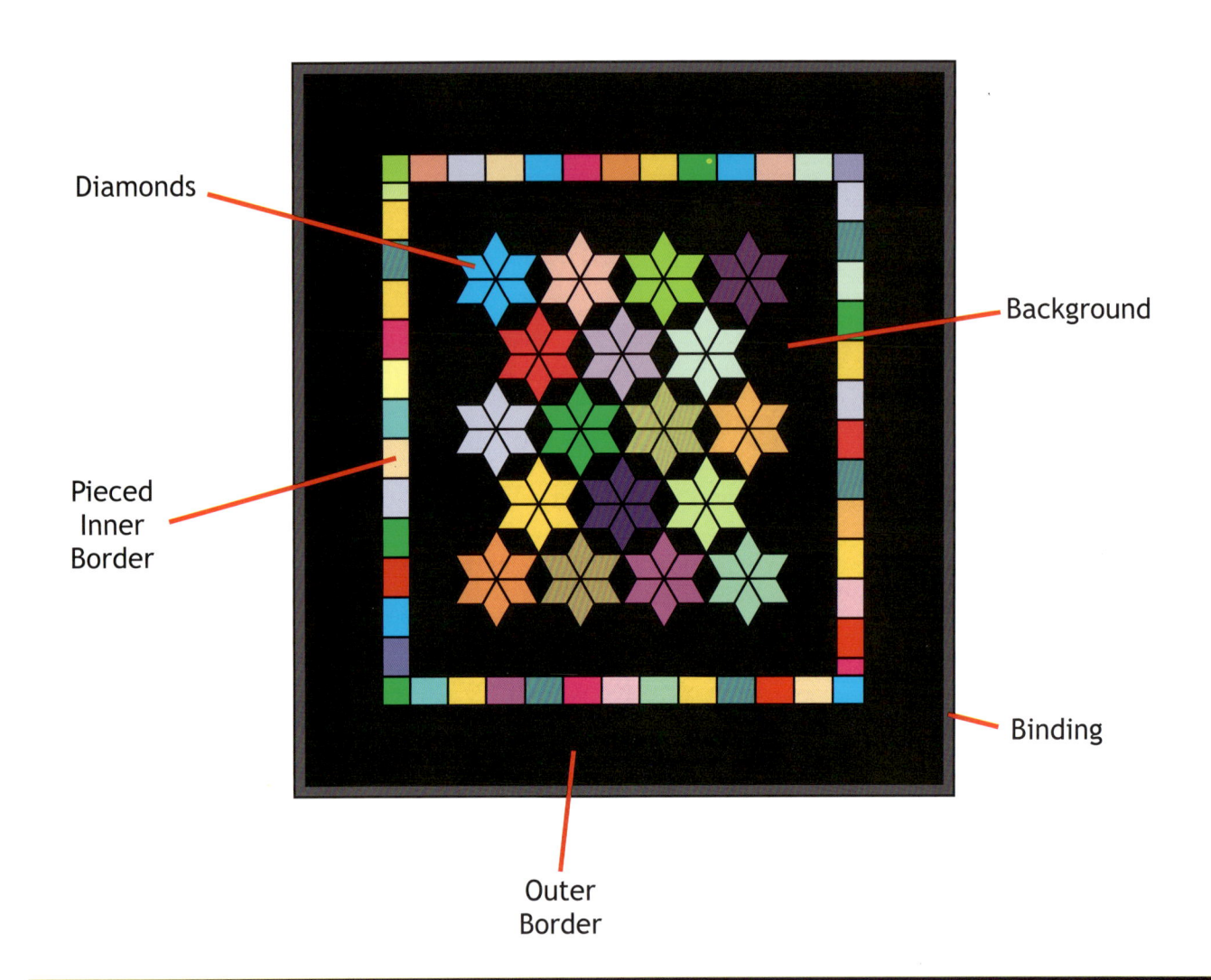

- Diamonds
- Background
- Pieced Inner Border
- Binding
- Outer Border

Borders

Stars In The Night includes a pieced inner border. The fabric used for it was left over after cutting the diamonds and also other scraps in the same colors. To create the same look simply sew scraps together to form a "strip" of fabric 1-1/2" wide. These "strips" can now be used the same as any plain border. Add the pieced inner border followed by the outer border. See instructions on page 50.

Quilting Recommendations

Stars In The Night was quilted with a stippled design in the background and the outer border.

Binding

Follow the instructions on page 52 for the French Fold method.

Mini Dresden Flowers

By Tess Herlan

Capture the splendor of petite flower blossoms all year round with this doll quilt.

Mini Dresden Flowers was pieced by Chris Welander and was quilted by Basket Cases of Clare, Illinois.

Mini Dresden Flowers

Piecing Pointers - Read all instructions before beginning

Fabric Required

Pieces	1/8 yard
Background and Backing	1 yard
Sashing	1/8 yard
Inner Border, Setting Squares, and Binding	1/4 yard
Outer Border	1/4 yard
Batting	20" x 27"

Miniature Wall Hanging

Quilt Size   18" x 25"

Paper Pieces Required

64 - Miniature Dresden Petals (DRE04)
8 - Small Circles

Piecing Pointers - Remember, this is a hobby and it's supposed to be fun!

Cutting Instructions

Pieces   **Note:** *A strip is considered the width of the fabric from selvage to selvage.*

If cutting from strips:
    Cut (3) 1-1/2" strips and then sub cut into (64) 1-1/2" squares for the Miniature Dresden Petals.
    Cut (1) 2" strip and then sub cut into (8) 2" squares for small circles.

If piecing out your stash:
    Cut (8) 1-1/2" x 1-1/2" squares of EACH color for the 8 Miniature Dresden Plates. (Fig.3)

Background
Cut (1) 4-1/2" strip and then sub cut into (8) 4-1/2" squares for background squares.
Cut (1) 7-3/4" strip and then sub cut into (2) 7-3/4" squares.
    Cut (2) 7-3/4" squares on both diagonals to form (8) side triangles.
Cut (1) 5" strip and then sub cut into (2) 5" squares.
    Cut (2) 5" squares on the diagonal to form corner triangles.

Sashing
Cut (3) 1" strips and then sub cut into (24) 1" x 4-1/2" rectangles for sashing borders.

Setting Squares   Cut (1) 1" strip and then sub cut into (17) 1" squares.

Inner Border   Cut (2) 1" strips.

Outer Border   Cut (2) 2-1/2" strips.

Backing   Cut a 19" x 25" rectangle.

Binding   Cut (3) 2-1/2" strips.

Assembly Instructions

1) Baste the fabric to the Paper Pieces according to the basic instructions.

2) Sew sets of two Miniature Dresden Petals together to make a quarter plate. (Fig.1)

3) Sew two quarter plates together, making one half of the plate. (Fig.2)

4) Sew the two halves together. Appliqué the circle to the center. (Fig.3)

Fig. 1
Make 32

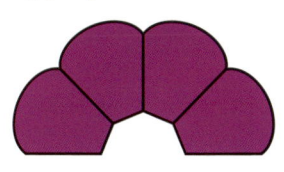

Fig. 2
Make 16

Fig. 3
Make 8

5) Appliqué the completed plate to the background square. See instructions on page 50. (Fig.4) Remove papers. See instructions on page 50.

Fig. 4
Make 8

6) Sew two of the 1" x 4-1/2" sashing strips to each side of Fig. 4. (Fig.5)

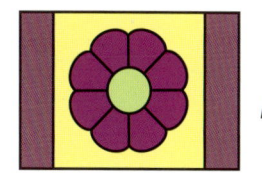

Fig. 5
Make 6

7) Make two rows of three blocks by sewing two Fig. 5 panels to each side of one Fig. 4 panel. (Fig.6)

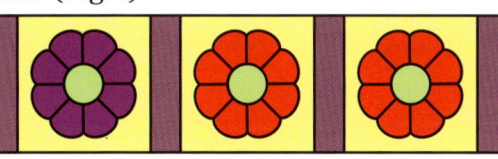

Fig. 6
Make 2

8) Sew the following sashing rows with setting squares.

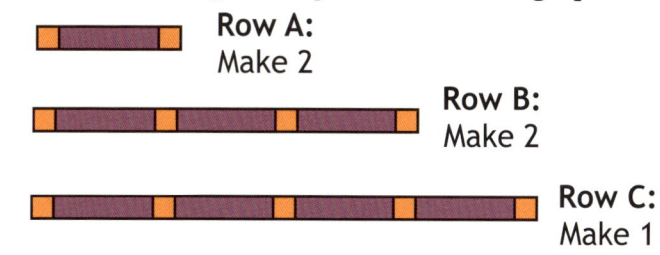

Row A: Make 2

Row B: Make 2

Row C: Make 1

9) Sew the rows of blocks and the sashing rows together. (Fig.7)

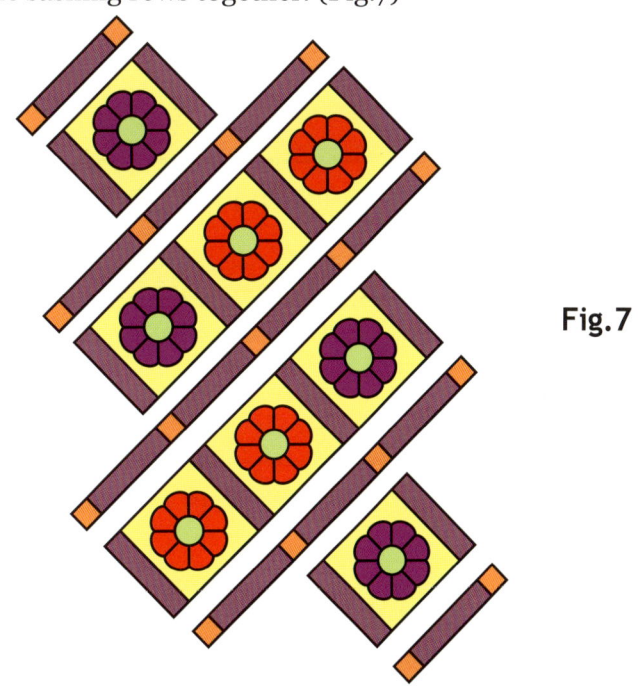

Fig. 7

Assembly Instructions Continued

10) Sew side and corner triangles to fill in the sides and corners of the top.

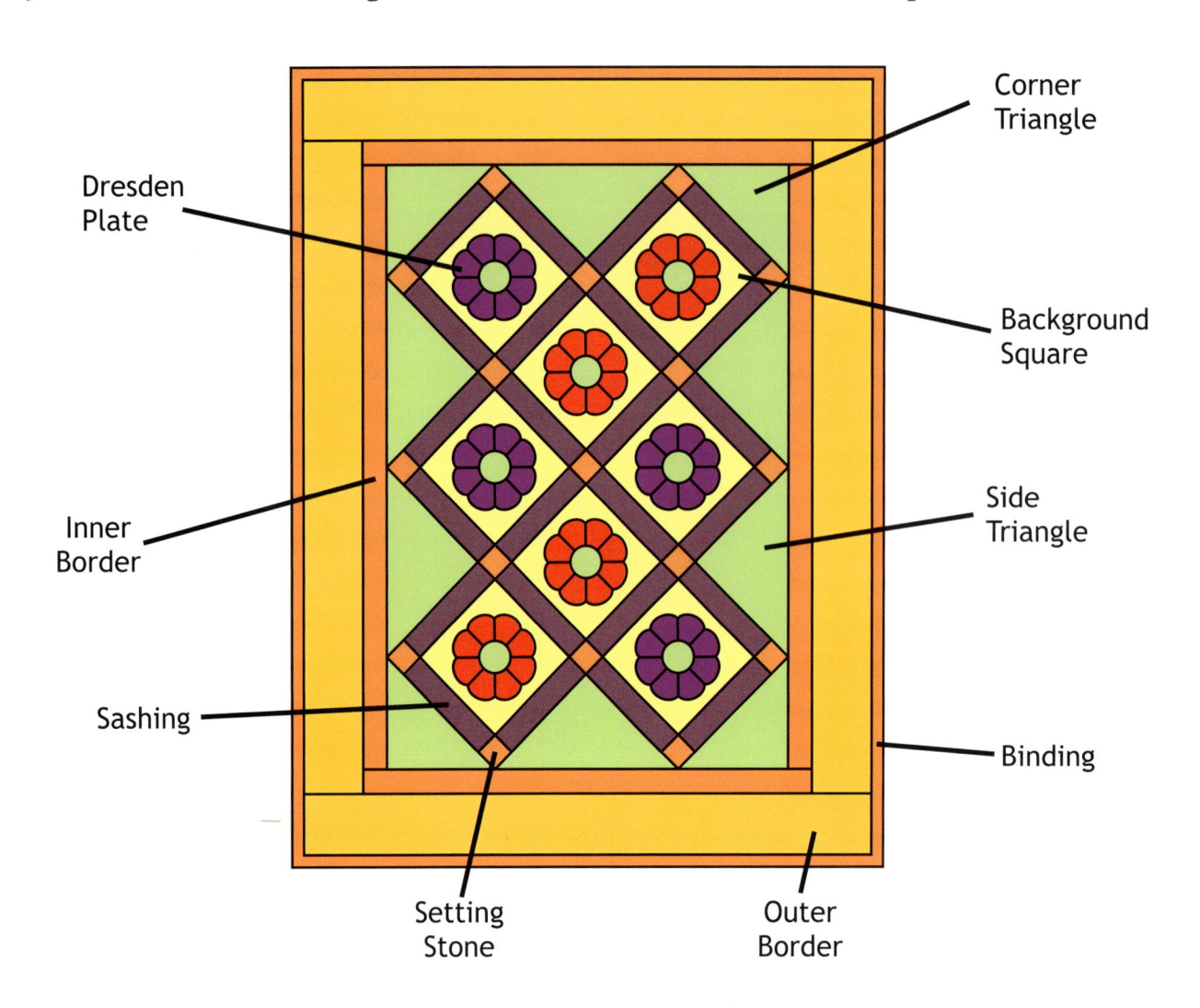

Borders

Add inner and outer borders. See instructions on page 50.

Quilting Recommendations

Mini Dresden Flowers was quilted in the ditch for the center. Then quilted with a stippled design in the outer border.

Binding

Follow the instructions on page 52 for the French Fold method.

Just Crazy

By Chris Moline

Piece out your stash for this really fun and just a bit crazy doll quilt. Any scraps will work to create this unique quilt!

Just Crazy was completed with invisible ties by Chris Moline.

Just Crazy

Piecing Pointers – Read all instructions before beginning

Miniature Wall Hanging

Quilt Size   13-1/2" x 16-1/2"

Paper Pieces Required

12 - 3" Squares (SQU300)

Fabric Required

Pieces	Assorted Scraps: 1/2 yard
Inner Border	1-1/4 yard of grosgrain ribbon
Outer Border	1/4 yard of black velvet
Backing	16" x 20"
Batting	16" x 20"
Optional	Assorted ribbons, lace, buttons, or other embellishments

Piecing Pointers – Leave all the papers in until the top is complete and the ribbon border is attached. This will keep the quilt top square and easy to manage.

Cutting Instructions

Pieces

As this quilt is very scrappy, we recommend the following approach to cutting the fabric for the pieces of the squares. Pin the Paper Pieces to the fabric and roughly trim around it allowing for a 1/2" seam allowance.

Assembly Instructions

1) Start by using a straight edge and a rotary cutter to create 4-6 custom shapes out of a 3" square. (Fig. 1) Mark the back side of these custom shapes with the block number so they do not get mixed up with other blocks or get reversed. (Fig. 2)

Fig.1

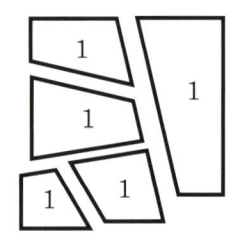

Fig.2

Piecing Pointers – It's easy to get pieces confused once they are cut. Keep the pieces organized by cutting one square at a time and immediately placing them in their own plastic bag or container.

34

Assembly Instructions Continued

2) Baste the fabric to the Paper Pieces according to the basic instructions. Using clips can help hold slippery fabric in place and can make basting easier.

3) Sew the custom Paper Pieces back together into their original squares. Create 12 blocks total.

4) Add embellishments to the individual blocks to give them depth and dimension. Ribbon and lace can be used in the block seams to emphasize the block divisions.

5) Sew blocks together to form 4 rows of 3 blocks.

6) Sew rows together to form the top.

7) Add the borders following the instructions for mitered corners on page 50.

8) Remove Papers. See instructions on page 49.

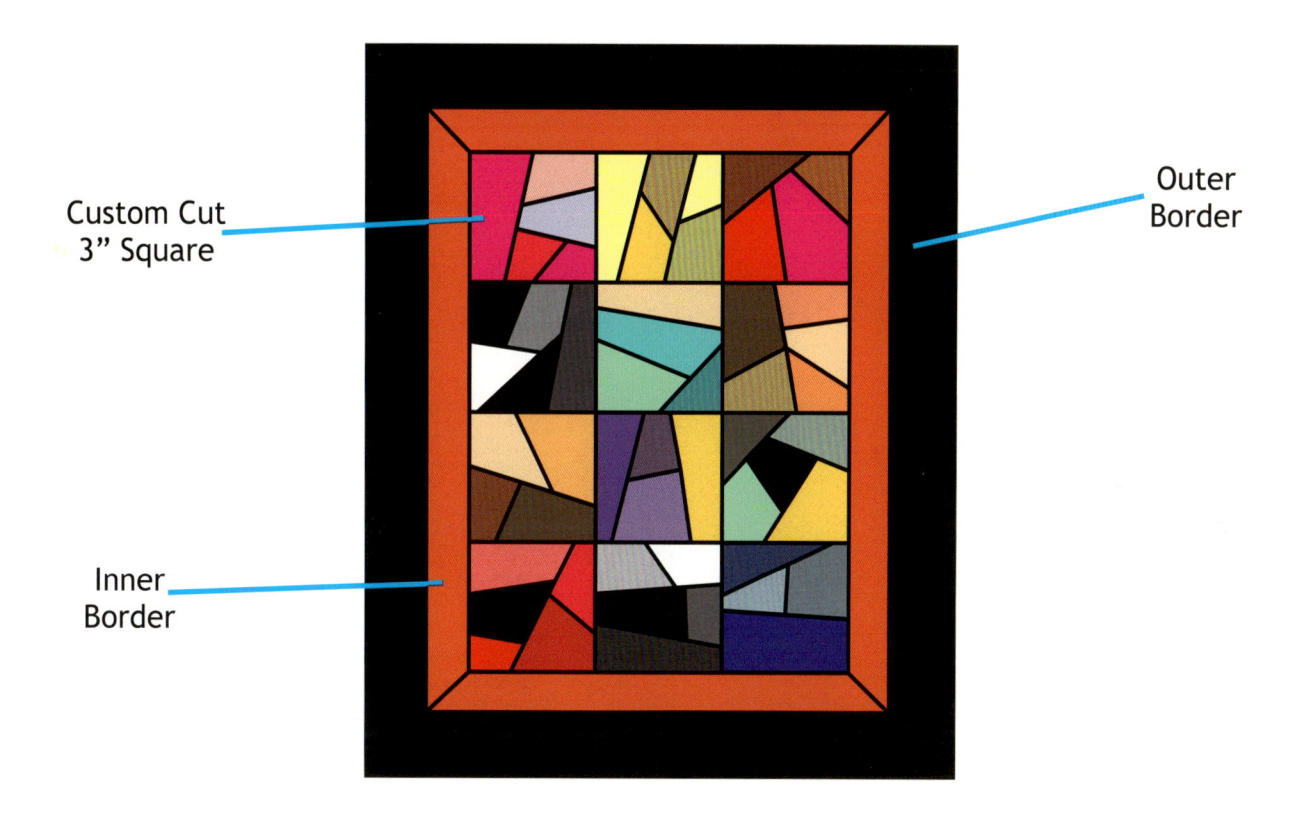

Custom Cut 3" Square

Outer Border

Inner Border

Quilt Tying Recommendations

Just Crazy was tied from the back at each block corner and not quilted. Begin by using 2 strands of contrasting or decorative thread in your needle. Place a finger near a block corner on the front to help locate where to put the stitch from the back side. Take a stitch through the back, catching only the seam allowances of the front and on through to the back. Leave approximately 3" of thread on the back side. Do not tie the ends together yet. Take another stitch to reinforce the tie. Cut the thread to approximately 3". Tie a square knot and trim the ends to 1/4". Repeat for each block corner.

Binding

Follow the instructions on page 52 for the knife edge method.

Hexagon Beauty

By Tess Herlan

A simple pattern can become an intriguing design by choosing the right color palette.

Hexagon Beauty was pieced by JoAnne Louis and quilted by Basket Cases of Clare, Illinois.

Hexagon Beauty

Piecing Pointers – Read all instructions before beginning

Wall Hanging

Quilt Size	16" x 18-1/2"

Paper Pieces Required

18 - 1" Hexagons (HEX100)
124 - 1" Half Hexagons (HHX100)

Fabric Required

Pieces White*:	1/2 yard
Colors:	1/2 yard of assorted scraps see details below
Background*	16" x 18-1/2"
Backing*	20" x 24"
Batting	20" x 24"
Binding	1/8 yard

*Same Fabric

Cutting Instructions

Pieces **Note:** A strip is considered the width of the fabric from selvage to selvage.

If cutting from strips:
Cut (2) 2-1/2" strips and then sub cut into (18) 2-1/2" x 2-1/2" squares for the hexagons.
Cut (8) 2-1/2" strips and then sub cut into (124) 2-1/2" x 3" rectangles for the half hexagons.

If piecing out your stash:
Cut (18) 2-1/2" x 2-1/2" squares for the hexagons.
Cut (6) 2-1/2" x 3" rectangles of EACH color for the half hexagons.

Binding Cut (2) 2-1/2" strips.

Assembly Instructions

1) Baste the fabric to the Paper Pieces according to the basic instructions.

2) Sew the following pieces together. (Fig.1 and Fig.2)

Fig.1 Make 18

Fig.2 Make 4

3) Sew Fig. 1 and Fig. 2 together to make the following rows.

Row A: Make 3

Row B: Make 2

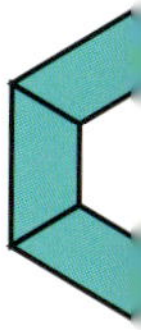

37

Assembly Instructions Continued

4) Starting at the top, whipstitch all of the rows together starting with Row A followed by Row B. Continue to alternate rows until completed.

5) Appliqué to background. See instructions on page 50.

6) Remove Papers. See instructions on page 50.

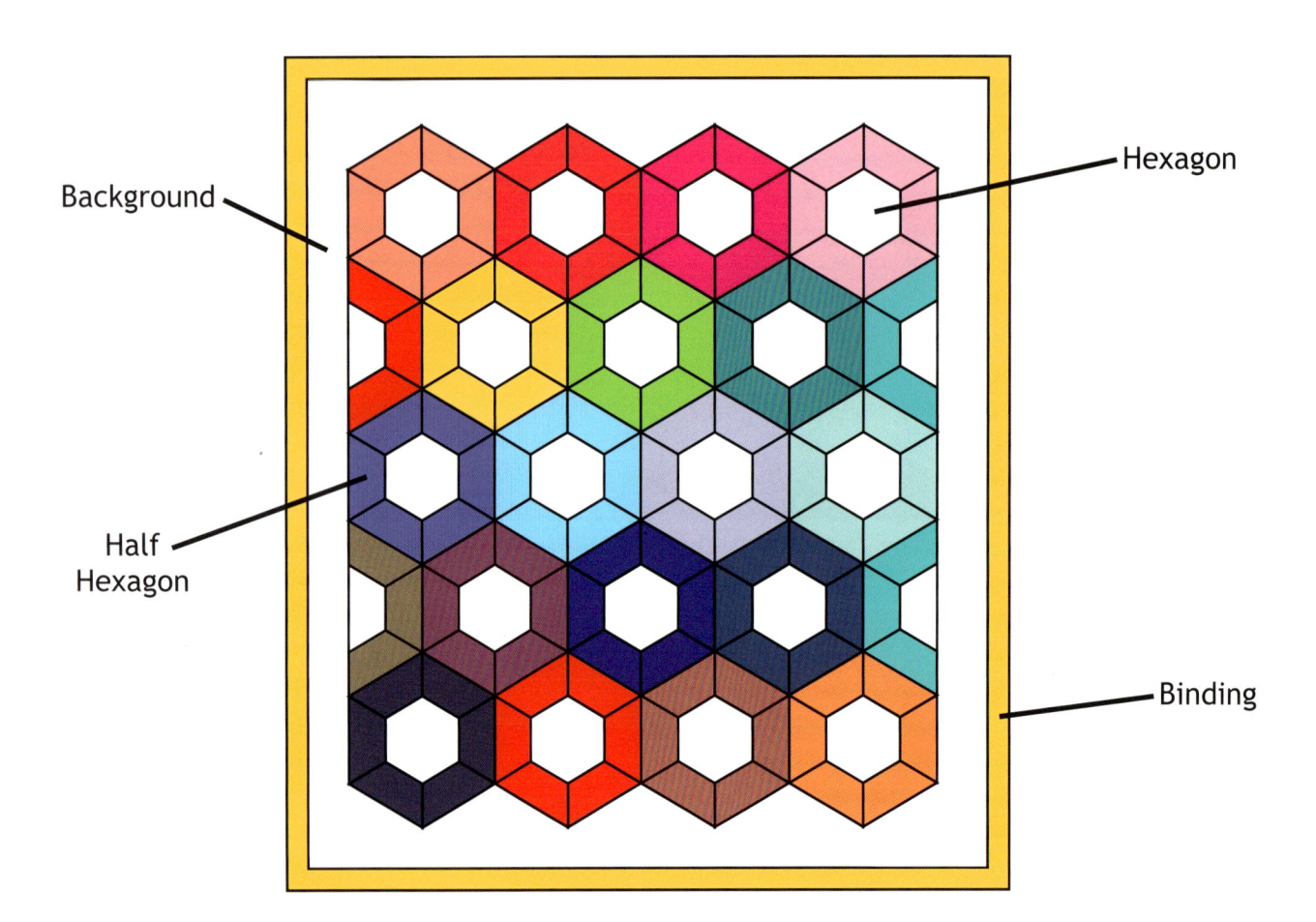

Diagram labels: Background, Half Hexagon, Hexagon, Binding

Quilting Recommendations

Hexagon Beauty was quilted in the ditch around the hexagons and half hexagons to make them stand out. It was echo quilted in the background.

Binding

Follow the instructions on page 52 for the French Fold method.

38

Perennial Posies

By Chris Moline

Set the table for your dollies using this original design in your favorite color combination.

Perennial Posies was quilted by Chris Moline with Superior Threads. The batting used was Pellon's Legacy.

Perennial Posies

Piecing Pointers - Read all instructions before beginning

Wall Hanging

Quilt Size   29-1/2" x 29-1/2"

Paper Pieces Required

20 - 2-3/4" Leaves (LEAF)
16 - 4" S-Leaves (SLEAF)
5 - 1" Squares (SQU100)
44 - 1" Pentagons (PEN100)

Fabric Required

Pieces	Green: 1/4 yard Red: 1/4 yard Yellow: 1/8 yard
Background	7/8 yard
Backing	32-1/2" x 32-1/2"
Batting	32-1/2" x 32-1/2"
Binding	1/4 yard
Bias Tape	1/4 yard of fabric OR 1-1/4 yards of 1/2" pre-made

Cutting Instructions

Pieces   **Note:** *A strip is considered the width of the fabric from selvage to selvage.*

Green: Cut (2) 2-1/2" strips and then sub cut into (16) 2-1/2" x 4-1/2" rectangles for the s-leaves.
        Cut (1) 2" strip and then sub cut into (4) 2" x 3-1/2" rectangles for the leaves.
Red: Cut (2) 2" strips and then sub cut into (16) 2" x 3-1/2" rectangles for the leaves.
        Cut (2) 2" strips and then sub cut into (40) 2" squares for the pentagons.
Yellow: Cut (1) 2" strips and then sub cut into (9) 2" squares for the pentagons and squares.

Background   Cut a 30-1/2" x 30-1/2" square.

Binding   Cut (4) 1-3/4" strips.

Assembly Instructions

1) Baste the fabric to the Paper Pieces according to the basic and curved instructions.

2) Sew the pentagons and squares into the following flowers. (Fig.1 and Fig.2)

Fig.1
Make 4

Fig.2
Make 5

40

Assembly Instructions Continued

3) Create bias tape stems. See page 52 for instructions. Make four 6-1/2" stems and four 4-1/2" stems.

4) Pin bias stems in place until you are satisfied with the placement. Pin green leaves and flowers to the stems in the center. Pin S-leaves and red leaves around the center to create the leaf border. See diagram below for placement. Appliqué everything in place. See instructions for appliqué on page 50.

5) Square off to 29" x 29".

6) Remove papers. See instructions on page 50.

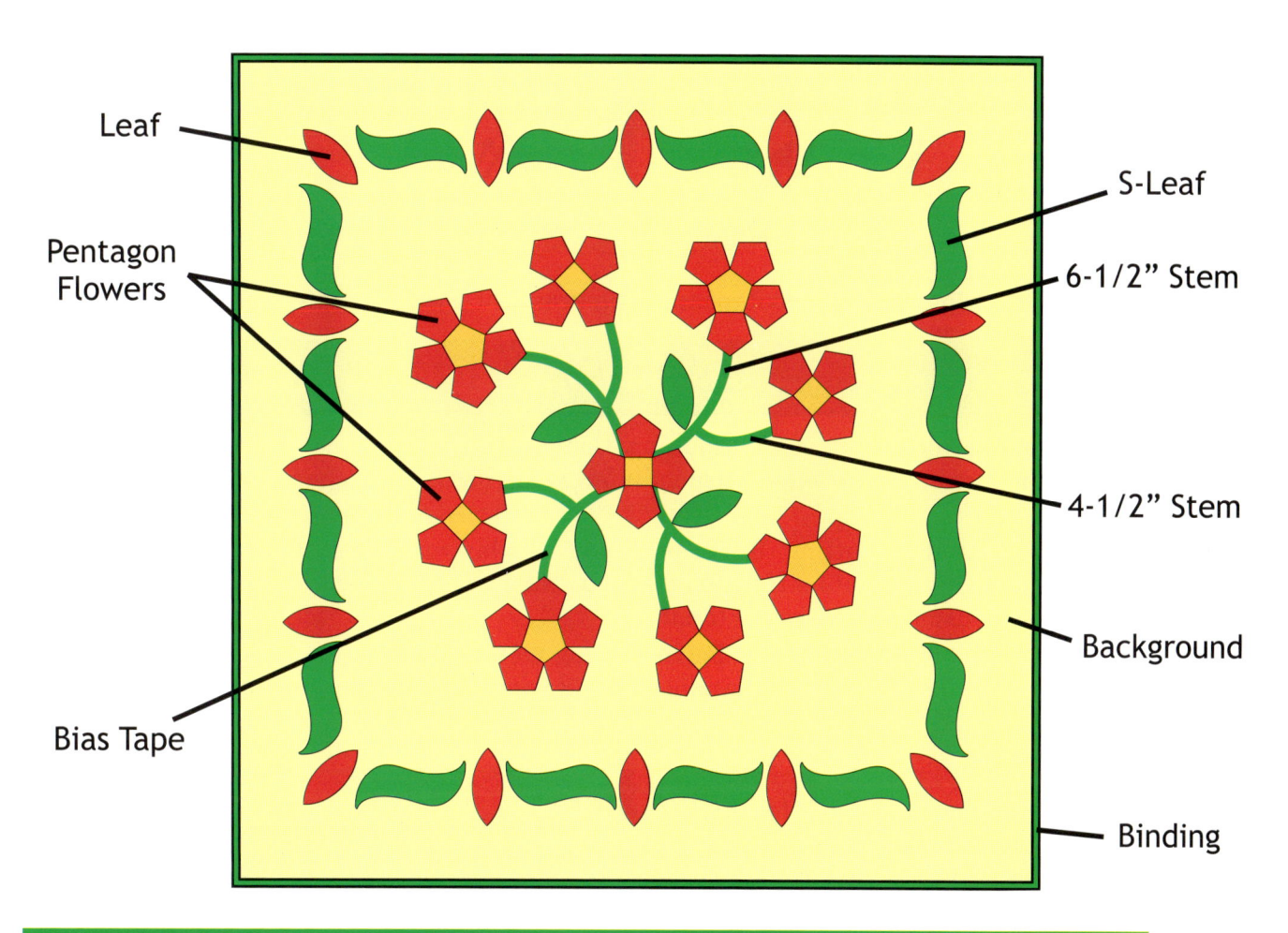

Labels on diagram: Leaf, Pentagon Flowers, Bias Tape, S-Leaf, 6-1/2" Stem, 4-1/2" Stem, Background, Binding

Quilting Recommendations

Perennial Posies was quilted with a stippled design throughout the entire background.

Binding

Follow the instructions on page 52 for the French Fold method.

English Paper Piecing

English Paper Piecing is a method of quilt making that has been in use for over 300 years. The accuracy, ease of use, and portability of projects has kept this method of quilt making popular throughout the years. The great thing about English Paper Piecing is that it allows you to carry a project with you at all times! You can piece in airplanes, in waiting rooms, at hospitals, at sporting events, and traveling in the car (as long as you are not driving of course!). If you have a few minutes, you can easily take it out and work on it. No need for a special place in your house where the sewing machine can be set up. You can have a basket of fabric and Paper Pieces by the sofa or your favorite chair. Perhaps this is why we love it so much. Though we have a warning for you – it's ADDICTIVE!

Measuring Paper Pieces

| We measure our Hexagons by **ONE** of the 6 sides | We measure our Diamonds by **ONE** of the 4 sides | We measure our Equilateral Triangles by **ONE** of the 3 sides | We measure our Leaves by the height of the piece |

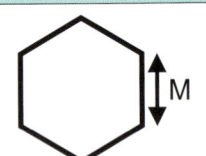

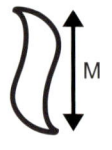

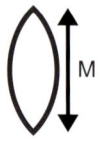

For more information about measuring pieces visit www.paperpieces.com

Cutting Fabric

This is JoAnne's least favorite part of quilt making. Could it be that she's more than a little afraid of her rotary cutter after an unfortunate accident a few years back? We'll spare you the gory details….

We get a lot of questions about cutting. The easy answer is to lay your paper piece on your "gridded" cutting mat and cut the fabric into strips using a seam allowance between ¼" and ½". More seam allowance is better and usually much easier to cut.

One of the great things about the English Paper Piecing method is that you don't have to be 100% accurate in your cutting. This is because the paper piece is your finished size. The fabric just has to be big enough to fold over and baste.

Piece Out Your Stash©

Scrap quilts are wonderful and perfect for English Paper Piecing, but organizing all those lovely fabric scraps can be daunting. We recommend this method to speed up the cutting process:
Sort the scraps into piles of similar sizes, i.e. 2" strips, 4" squares, etc. Then you can stack several pieces and cut the shape needed. (Give yourself permission to toss out the teeny-tiny leftovers!)

Look for the symbol to find quilts where you can Piece Out Your Stash ©!

Cutting For Hexagons

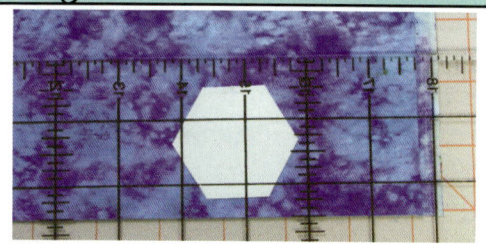

1) Place your hexagon on the cutting mat to see what size strip you need to cut. In this case, a 1" hexagon will take a 2-1/2" strip.

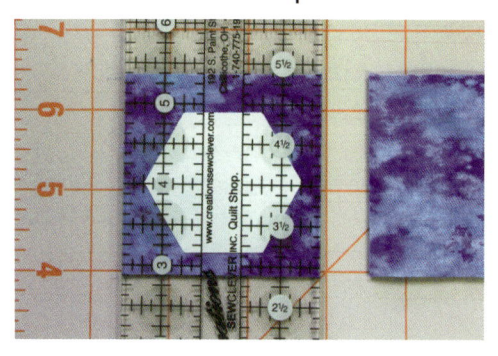

2) Sub cut the 2-1/2" strips into 2-1/2" Squares. The ONLY time we cut fabric hexagons instead of squares is for fussy cutting.

Cutting For Diamonds

1) Cut the strips for your diamonds as described above for hexagons. Place your diamond on the cutting mat and allow 1/4" to 1/2" from the top and bottom of the piece.

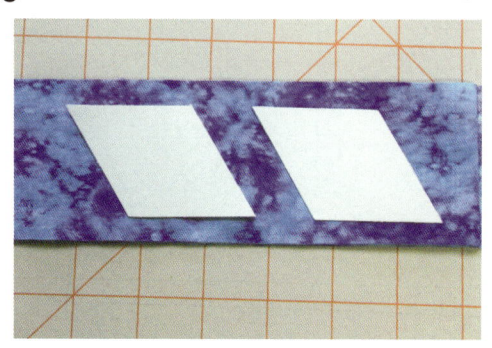

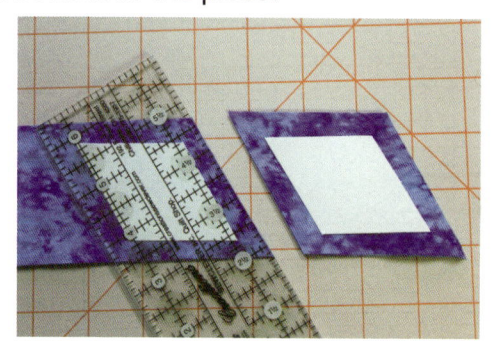

2) After cutting the strips, use the 60 degree angle for 6 point diamonds or 45 degree angle for 8 point diamonds on your ruler and sub cut the strips into diamond shapes.

Cutting For Triangles

1) Cut the strips for your triangles as described above for hexagons. Place your triangle on the cutting mat and allow 1/4" to 1/2" from the top and bottom of the piece.

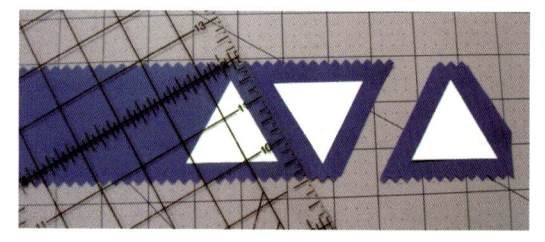

2) After cutting the strips, use the 60 degree angle on your ruler and sub cut the strips into triangle shapes.

Basting

This is one of the best parts about English Paper Piecing, because it is so mindless and you can baste just about anywhere!

There are two schools of thought about basting. John Welander calls them the "Holey Wars - To Pierce or not to Pierce". This refers to sewing through the paper or catching the corners. JoAnne freely admits that she is biased toward sewing through the paper. She finds this is the fastest and most secure method of basting. Over the years when someone is having problems basting it is usually because they are NOT sewing through the paper. Chris prefers a "half breed" method. She sews through the papers except for straight sides less than ¾". Then she only tacks the corners. If you have success with one method over another, it's fine. There are no quilt police!

Simple Basting

1) Place and pin the Paper Piece to the wrong side of the fabric. Cut at least 1/4" larger than the Paper Piece. We cut squares from the fabric for hexagon pieces. This gives you more fabric to turn over, allowing you to easily baste without fussing with only 1/4" of fabric.

2) Fold the seam allowance over the Paper Piece and baste into this position using big stitches. When basting pointed shapes, let your "tails" wag. When appliquéing, tuck the tail under the piece so you get sharp points.

3) Place right sides together and overcast pieces together with small whip stitches, just catching edges of fabric. We recommend around 6 - 10 stitches per inch.

4) When you have another piece sewn to **all** sides, remove the basting and take out the Paper Piece. You can reuse the Paper Piece.

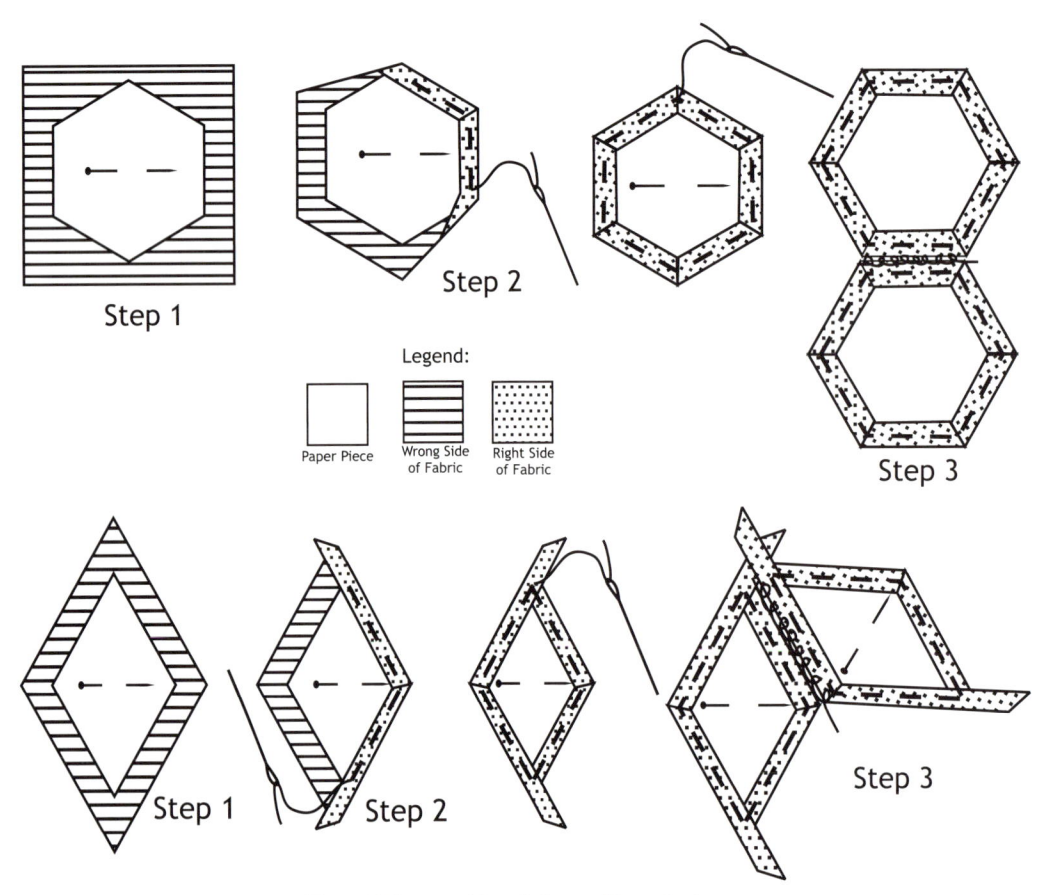

Step 1 — Step 2 — Step 3

Legend:
Paper Piece | Wrong Side of Fabric | Right Side of Fabric

Step 1 — Step 2 — Step 3

Use this method for all points.

44

Chain Basting

Once you have the hang of basting, (after about 5 pieces) you can start chain basting. Julie Griffis taught us this method! Just baste the first piece and then leave a few inches of thread before starting to baste the next piece. Continue until you run out of thread. If the pieces start to tangle, just snip them apart.

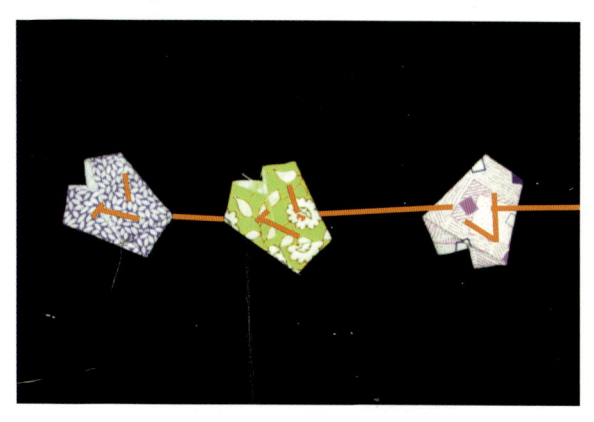

Start of Chain Basting

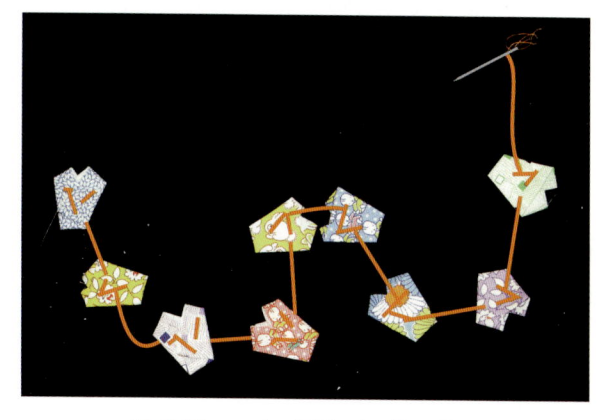

Full Thread of Chain Basting

Basting Curves

English Paper Piecing is a great way to get a smooth edge on curved pieces. When doing an inner curve you will need to clip the curve. On outer curves it will depend on how tight the curve is, sometimes you can just fold over and baste as usual, on other pieces you start a running stitch in the fabric only at the beginning of the curve and gather the fabric. See the following steps for clarification.

Basting Inner Curves

1) Pin paper piece to fabric.

2) Clip the fabric on the inner curve.

3) Fold the fabric over and baste as usual.

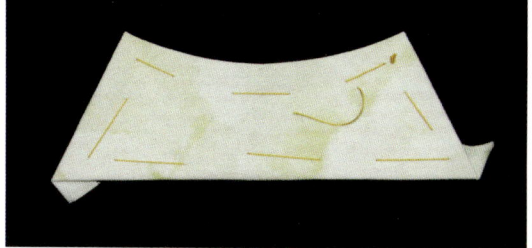

4) Finish basting the paper piece.

Basting Outer Curves

Legend:
- Paper Piece
- Wrong Side of Fabric
- Right Side of Fabric

1) Fold the seam allowance over the paper piece, starting just above the point of the heart. Baste through the paper until you reach the curve. Going outside the paper about 1/8", do a small running stitch through just the fabric around the curve to the inside point.

2) Clip fabric into the point, stopping about 1/16" from the paper piece. Take one basting stitch at the point through the fabric and the paper piece. Gently pull the thread and the fabric will wrap around the curved edge of the paper.

3) Once again do a running stitch through the fabric only, around the second curve. Baste through the fabric and paper on the straight edge, pulling the thread to shape the fabric to the second curve.

4) Fold seam allowance over the paper to form the point and baste around point to your starting place. Take one extra basting stitch past the beginning point. Clip thread. It is not necessary to fasten the thread off.

CAUTION: If you are using up odd thread, make sure it is colorfast. This is easy to do, just rub the thread on white fabric. If there is any staining, throw the thread away!

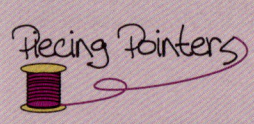

Piecing Pointers
- Use contrasting thread when basting. This makes for easier removal later. Start with the knot on the right side of the fabric. This makes it easier to remove the basting.

Whip Stitching
Whip Stitching Straight Edges

This is Chris's favorite part – seeing those many pieces come together as a whole block or top.
After you have a number of pieces basted you can start whipping them together. With a matching thread, bury the knot between the paper piece and the seam allowance. If sewing a dark and light colored piece together, match the thread to the darker color.

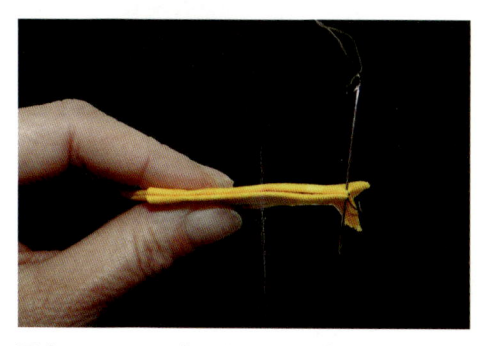

Take two anchoring stitches when starting and whip stitch until you reach the next corner. Do not sew through the paper when joining the pieces. Your needle should slide next to the paper between the edge of the paper piece and the fabric, just catching the edge of the fabric.

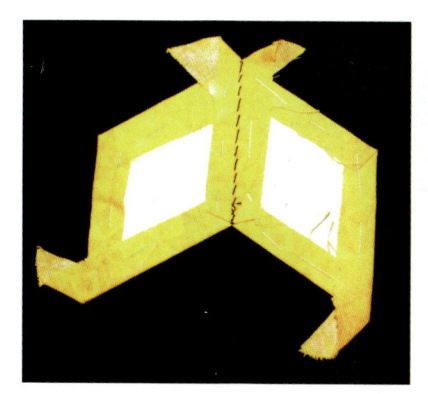

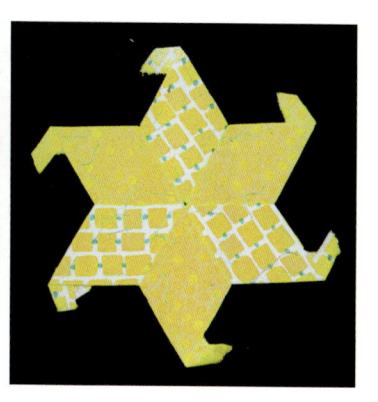

We recommend about 6-10 stitches per inch. When you reach the "corner", secure it by taking two stitches together. If your whip stitches are showing on the right side of the fabric, tighten the stitch slightly and catch less fabric. The stitching should be taut and even, but not pulling. Continue whipping pieces together to finish the block.

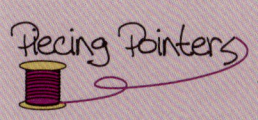

Piecing Pointers – If you are working on pieces less than an inch per side, you can travel the thread along the seam allowance and start whipping at a new point.

47

Whip Stitching Curves Together

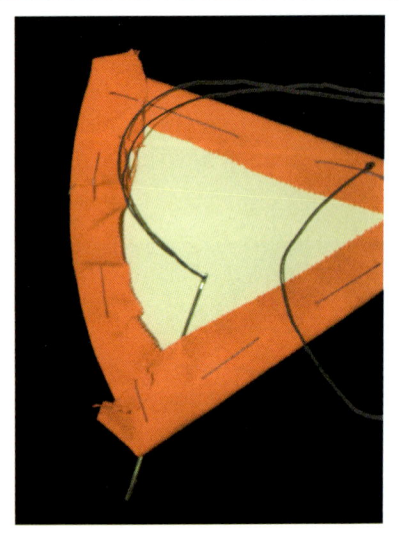

1) Once both curved pieces are basted, whip stitch the outer curve to the inner curve. Start by going through the corner of the outer curve.

2) Complete the stitch by going though the corner of the inner curve while keeping both pieces flat.

3) Continue to whip stitch the pieces together. Make sure to catch only the fabric and not the paper.

4) Finish your whip stitch around the whole curve to finish the piece.

Removing the Paper Pieces

This is the second favorite part for both JoAnne and Chris because the quilt top looks so different after removing the basting threads. While you can leave all the papers in your piece until you are done, Paper Pieces can also be reused many times. For some of these projects where a large number of Paper Pieces are required, we recommend removing papers once a piece is completely surrounded. If you are a "corner catcher" you don't have to remove the basting stitches, just pull the papers from the wrong side. To remove the basting stitches, use a pin or tweezers to pull the threads out. (Remember this is AFTER a piece is surrounded on all sides with other pieces.) If the basting doesn't come out easily try using bigger stitches next time.

1) Cut and gently pull out basting stitches. Before you remove the paper, trim the excess seam allowance if you are worried about the bulk of the excess fabric or if you plan to hand quilt.

2) Gently pull out the Paper Piece.

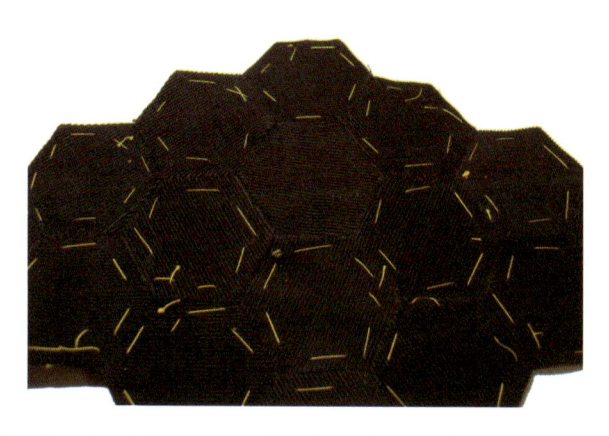

3) Continue to remove the paper pieces, remembering to take out only the pieces that are surrounded on all sides.

Piecing Pointers - Our Paper Pieces are reusable 3-10 times. If they get too crumpled you can "freshen" them up with a DRY iron.

Appliqué

English Paper Piecing makes appliqué easy. Start by pinning your basted shape onto the background fabric. Appliqué the piece to the background fabric using a blind stitch. The edge of the paper piece will act as a guide, allowing you to catch only the edge of the fabric as you blind stitch it to the background.

Appliquéing Quilt Tops To A Background

After you have finished the quilt top, appliqué it onto the background fabric. We recommend buying extra wide fabric or piecing the background fabric together to reach the dimension stated in the pattern. This requires more fabric, however it is much easier to finish the quilt this way. To begin, first baste the quilt top onto the background fabric. This prevents slipping and bunching of the fabric when appliquéing. After you baste the top down, appliqué it down using a blind stitch.

Removing Papers From Appliqué Pieces

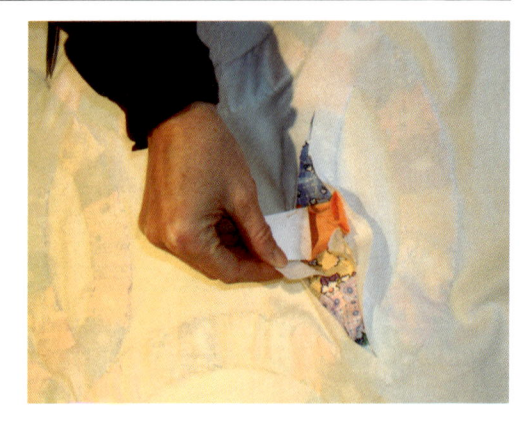

Once you have completed your appliqué, turn to the back side and cut the background fabric 1/4" inside the applique stitching lines and remove it. (It is easy to do as the papers will keep you from cutting through the front fabric.) Pull the basting threads and remove the papers from the back side. These papers can be used again.

Adding Borders

Squaring It Off

To add a straight border you must first trim the edges of your quilt top. Remove all the pieces and press the outside seam allowances flat. Take your rotary cutter and ruler and trim all the edges to get a straight line a 1/4" away from the edge. If this is going to interfere with your design, you might want to piece another row of the design around the edge so you won't lose the pattern.

1) Line up your ruler 1/4" from the edge of the top.

2) Trim the excess.

3) Remove cut pieces and continue for all sides of the quilt top.

Cutting Square Borders

Once your quilt top is squared off, measure the long side of your quilt. Add 4" to this number to get the total for your long borders. Cut two borders this size. Match the middles of the borders with the middle of the quilt top and pin borders in place. Sew them to your quilt top (Fig. 1). Repeat the process for the short borders. (Fig. 2). Once both sets of borders are attached, square off the corners and trim away any excess bulk from behind. (Fig. 3).

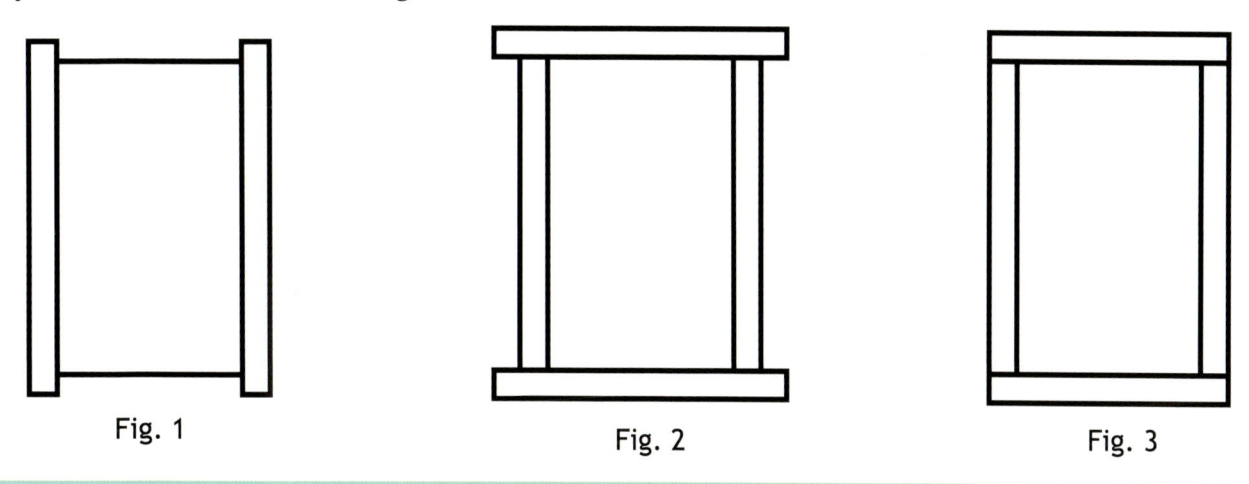

Fig. 1

Fig. 2

Fig. 3

Cutting Mitered Borders

Once your quilt top is squared off, measure the long side of your quilt. Take this number plus twice the width of the border to be added and 2" to get a sufficient length. Cut two strips this size for the long borders. Repeat the process on the short side and cut 2 short borders. Center the border strips and pin in place. To create mitered corners sew the borders to the quilt top leaving a 1/4" from the edge at the beginning and end of the strip. Place your quilt top on an ironing board right side up. Fold the ends of the border strips back onto themselves with the right sides together to create a 45 degree angle. Press to get sharp creases. (Fig 4) With the right sides together, fold your quilt on the diagonal. Align the borders along the crease and pin in place. Sew along the crease making sure to backstitch 1/4" at the seam so no gaps form. (Fig. 5) Press the seam open to check that the corner is lined up. (Fig. 6) When border is complete trim the excess fabric 1/4" from the sewing line. Repeat for remaining corners.

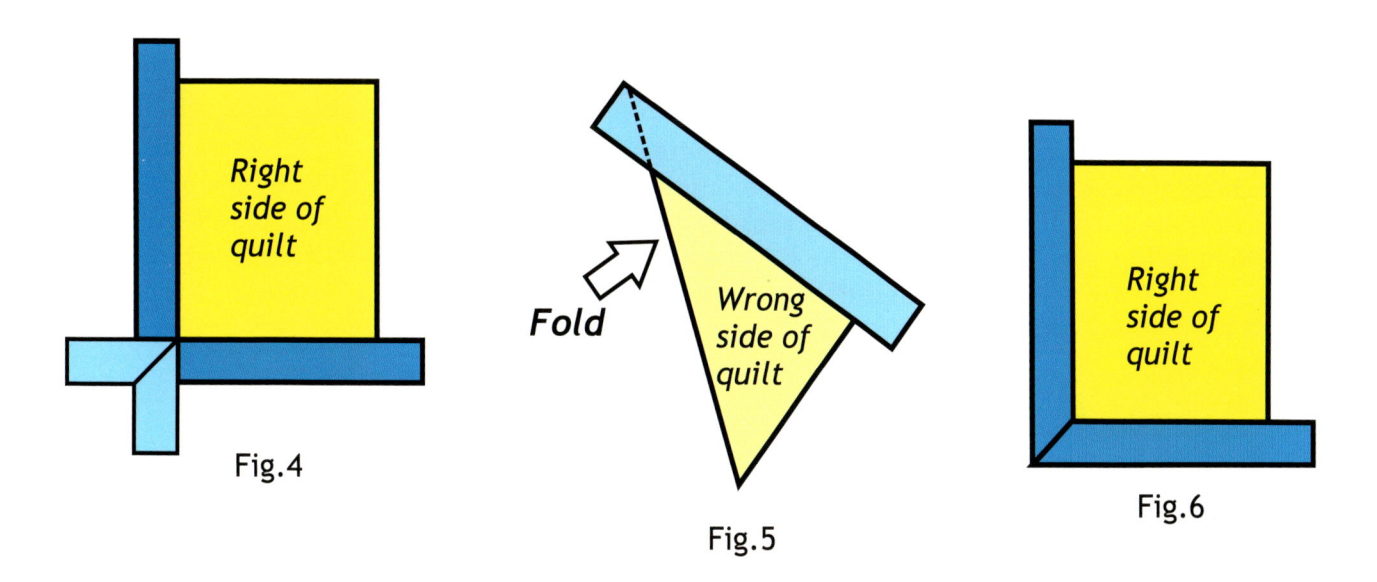

Fig.4

Fig.5

Fig.6

Bias Tape

Make bias tape for all your flower stems. Beginning 12" from one end of the fabric, cut 1" wide strips on a 45 degree angle. (Fig. 1) Fold and press your strip in thirds. Cut into the length(s) needed according to the pattern.

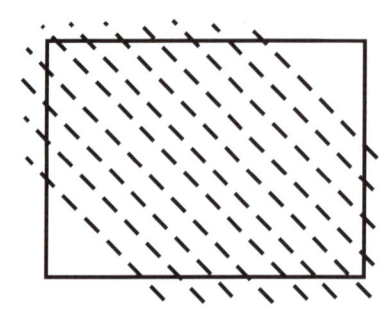

Fig. 1

Binding

French Fold/Double Binding

A French Fold or Double binding provides an outer frame or protected edge to your quilt. Binding can be cut on the straight of grain for straight sides or on the bias for irregular or scalloped edges.

JoAnne cuts all her bindings at 2 ½" then sews them on with her walking foot, as this is the perfect width for that foot. Chris cuts hers at 1 ¾" and sews them on with her quarter inch foot. Whichever strip width you choose, sew all your binding sections together using mitered seams to reduce bulk. Press in half lengthwise, wrong sides together, to double the binding. Beginning about 12" from any corner, align the cut edges of the binding with the outer edge of the quilt on the front and sew in place using the edge of your machine foot as a guide from the outside edge. Miter your corners when turning.

When the binding is completely attached, clip the batting in the corners to reduce bulk, especially if you have used a thicker batting, so that your corners are sharp and angular. Turn the folded edge to the back and hand blind stitch in place.

Rickrack Binding

To insert rickrack into the binding, first cut the binding strips and sew them together, then sew the rickrack down the center of the right side of the binding using a small machine stitch length. Press the binding in half lengthwise with the rickrack to one side. Using the instructions for the French fold/double binding, sew the binding to the BACK of the quilt with the rickrack on top. When the binding is completely attached, turn the folded edge to the front, now only half of the rickrack will show and hand blind stitch taking a stitch between each rickrack bump.

Knife Edge/Self Finished Edge

If a knife or self finished edge is to be used, your quilting needs to end ½" from the outer edge of the quilt. Trim the batting ¼" inside the unfinished edge and fold the fabric from the top over the batting. Fold in ¼" of the back to the inside. Use an invisible hem stitch to secure the seam. A quilting line can also be added to finish the edge.

Portable Project Strategies
Packing Your Project For Work On The Road

The unique aspect of paper piecing is that it can be done almost anywhere, except under water! By packaging your blocks into zippered plastic bags, it allows you to account for all the segments. It also allows you to pick up a bag to take with you to the dentist, the service station, the doctor, the soccer game or even an airplane or on a road trip.

In addition to your bag of fabric and Paper Pieces, you will need a sewing kit. We recommend the following:

- Any small sharp scissors to cut thread and possibly trim your fabric pieces
- Thread - any color, if basting, or colors to match your fabrics
- Needles
- Clips (see information on page 55)
- A thimble (if you use one)
- Desktop Needle Threader (makes it so much easier)
- Dome Threaded Needle Case or Strawberry pincushion - to protect your needles and keep them clean

Pack all your bags into a project box large enough to hold all the parts. We often use plastic project boxes that have handles so that they are easy to tote along. As your top nears completion, you may need a larger bag to contain the folded top.

Finishing Touches

Batting

This is a topic covered in several books and by batting companies. Choose your batting to fit the project. To determine the batting you need, check with www.quiltlegacy.com for stitch spacing, loft and shrinkage.

The Quilt Sandwich

No matter how you slice it, you have to get the three layers together. For these small quilts, basting from corner to corner and side to side is usually sufficient to hold the layers together.

Embellishments

Beading or other embellishments on any of these quilts is totally optional, but can serve a lot of purposes. A little sparkle adds some interest to the surface and will draw your viewer in for a closer look. Beads in place of French knots and along the embroidery lines will add pizzazz to your project. You can also embroider in some extra details. Beading can also hide minor faults in quilting, appliqué or embroidery. Embellish it or not. It is your choice.

The Quilt Sleeve

If your project is going off to a show or going to hang on a wall, you will need a sleeve. We put permanent sleeves in most of our quilts using a 9" width of the backing fabric. Hem the ends to the appropriate width, fold in half lengthwise wrong sides together. On the backside pin the sleeve to the top edge of the quilt. By sewing the sleeve into the binding, your quilt will have complete stability across the entire width. Wait to appliqué the bottom side of the sleeve down until all the binding steps are completed.

Quilt Labels

Labels are very important. Give your quilt a nice name, add your name, location, date completed, source of inspiration and purpose for making. Make sure you acknowledge the source of your pattern and your quilter if you don't do it yourself. Affix the label on the lower left corner of the back. Whether your label is fancy or plain is up to you. Don't let your wonderful completed quilt become a poor "maker unknown" quilt of the future.

Appraising

Now for the most important part of all, since you have spent all this time on your masterpiece, please call an AQS Certified Appraiser of Quilted Textiles for a written Insurance Value appraisal. Your quilt is worth money. Probably more than you realize. Without a quilt appraisal, your quilt will be valued at the price of a cheap blanket. Protect your investment. To find an AQS Certified Appraiser call the American Quilter's Society at (270) 898-7903 or logon to the website for the Professional Association of Appraisers – Quilted Textiles at www.quiltappraisers.org . You will thank yourself for doing this.

Resources

Paper Pieces

All the quilts in this book are made with precision cut English Paper Pieces available from:
Paper Pieces
P. O. Box 68
Sycamore, IL 60178
1-800-337-1537
1-815-899-0925 (Outside USA)
www.paperpieces.com

Call for a FREE full color catalog. Wholesale inquiries welcome.

Needles, Thimbles, Singer Featherweight Attachments and Parts

Jean S. Lyle
P. O. Box 289,
Quincy, IL 62309-0289
www.jslyle.com

Our Favorite Notions

Superior Thread Frosted Donut

A bobbin ring will hold small amounts of all the thread colors that you may need for your project.

Nut Pick or Tweezers

For removing the smaller pieces, these handy tools will flip your papers out from the completely surrounded pieces.

Clips

Plastic clips, small alligator clips, toy plastic clothespins or mini binder clips will hold your fabrics to the pieces when you start basting or when you whipstitch pieces together.

Clover Desktop Needle Threader

Clover Needle Dome

55

Lectures and Workshops

Chris Moline has been an avid quilter for many years and has produced award winning quilts. Her quilt collection spans a variety of techniques, styles and experiences. As a certified quilt appraiser and experienced quilt restorer, her knowledge of quilting and fabric history is quite extensive. She presents several lectures and workshops designed to inspire quilters to learn more about quilts and quilting, stretch their creative ability, experiment with traditional as well as contemporary styles and techniques, and improve their productivity. Chris has lectured and provided workshops for the American Quilter's Society, museums, historical societies and quilt guilds for more than 20 years. Contact Chris at chrismoline@att.net for pricing and additional information.

Lectures

Quilt Project Management

An application of progressive project management techniques used in business to help you organize your quilting projects. Get more work done in less time; manage multiple projects. Set goals and meet them! Chris taught project management to employees of Fortune 500 companies for 10 years and her high quilt output is a testament to the use of this technique. She helps you apply skills you do not know that you have to your quilting projects. A quilt "show and tell" is included to prove the results.

English Paper Piecing

Featuring this time tested technique to create unique quilts; Chris shows antique and new quilts to inspire your creative juices. Included in this lecture are techniques for packaging your projects for travel and creating schedules for completing long-term heirloom projects. Whether scrappy or fabric based - Chris shows how to apply this technique to your quilt making repertoire.

Confronting Your Stash

A unique design approach which facilitates the use of "stash" fabrics in creating a new look in your quilts. Chris helps you find a way to let the fabric speak to you, telling you what to create, inspiring you to try new designs and patterns. This is a light-hearted, creative and interactive presentation. The audience is invited to bring their fabric challenges. Many completed quilt samples and a stash example to help viewers discover a whole new design inspiration waiting for them at home.

Other Lectures Include:

Collector's Diary (stories of quilt collectors), Quilt and Quilt Maker's Stories, Let's make better quilts! (learn how judges and appraiser view your quilts), Ugly Quilts (learn the important keys for creating quilts that please the eye), Exegesis- Greek for Interpret (your group's quilts are dated, discussed and assigned an insurance value range), Quilt Care And Cleaning, 200 Years of Quilt History, 19th Century Quilts – Trunk Show, 20th Century Quilts – Trunk Show, Quilt Restoration and Repair

Workshops

Basic English Paper Piecing
Advanced English Paper Piecing
Clues for Dating Quilts
Hand Piecing Basics
Intermediate Hand Piecing
Do-it-yourself Quilt Restoration and Repair
Hand Quilting
Raleigh - Learn the tricks of curved piecing by machine
Two Block Two Step - A unique setting technique can be used on other traditional blocks to make your quilt a one-of-a-kind design.
Appliqué Design for Non-Artists

About the Authors

JOANNE LOUIS

Everyone is known for something. I'd like to say I'm well known for my great beauty, or discovering a cure for some awful disease, but around here I'm known for making quilts (notice I didn't say prize winning quilts) and wacky shoes. Now I've been quilting longer than I've been collecting wacky shoes, but being a typical quilter I've given away most of my quilts, so it's safe to say there are more shoes in our house than quilts…(fabric, however, is a different story).

Being a known quilter, I have been asked many times how much I'd charge to make someone a quilt. My standard response is that I'd have to charge a couple of thousand dollars, but I'd be happy to teach you for free. After swooning from the shock, the excuses start: "I can't quilt, I can't sew, I hate to sew on the machine, I don't know how," (and my personal favorite) "I don't have the patience." I have managed to convince a few people to give it a try. My best successes have been ladies who have a working knowledge of a sewing machine. I figured out early-on that sewing machines are not my friend. (I still put my bobbins in upside down, and once sewed two whole quilts with the needle in backwards).

I guess I'm a low-tech gal in a high-tech world, because I have great success teaching people how to quilt using the old fashioned English Paper Piecing method.

CHRIS MOLINE

As a Certified Quilt Appraiser, I don't get to see many doll quilts, as most people think these little things don't have enough value to be appraised. But you might be surprised! So few of the antique ones survive and child made quilts are not often very sophisticated, but the fact that they have survived gives them value. They are often a reflection of the styles of quilts in the households that they come from and tell us a lot about the times and conditions for children in the past.

My sister has always been the doll maker in my family, but I just get so charged up making doll quilts. They can be quick and easy or lots of little pieces – it makes no difference to me. My first quilt was a doll quilt that I still have and treasure. Doll quilts are just so versatile. Hang them on the wall or give them to a child – they are always pleasing and fun.

If you haven't tried this age old method, we hope this book will inspire you to start quilting, and, if you are already addicted, that you will find new inspiration!

The Two of Us

Chris: "Who would take a box of little squares that nobody wanted and see a goldmine? Who would start a project with a deadline that is about 15 years out? In the process I met JoAnne Louis and found a kindred spirit and new friend or is it fiend? Someone who craves a challenge and is not afraid to do a challenging project (like a book or two) and make some of the quilts that we can think up. Someone who sees a pattern or a design and can take it to the next step to make it just that little bit more. Someone who is not afraid of color and can put the rainbow together with surprising results."

JoAnne and Chris met working in side by side booths at quilt shows and discovered a mutual passion for challenging projects and making quilts with a bit of whimsy. Some might say we are an odd pair, but we complement each other – all the more fun!!

All Dolled Up

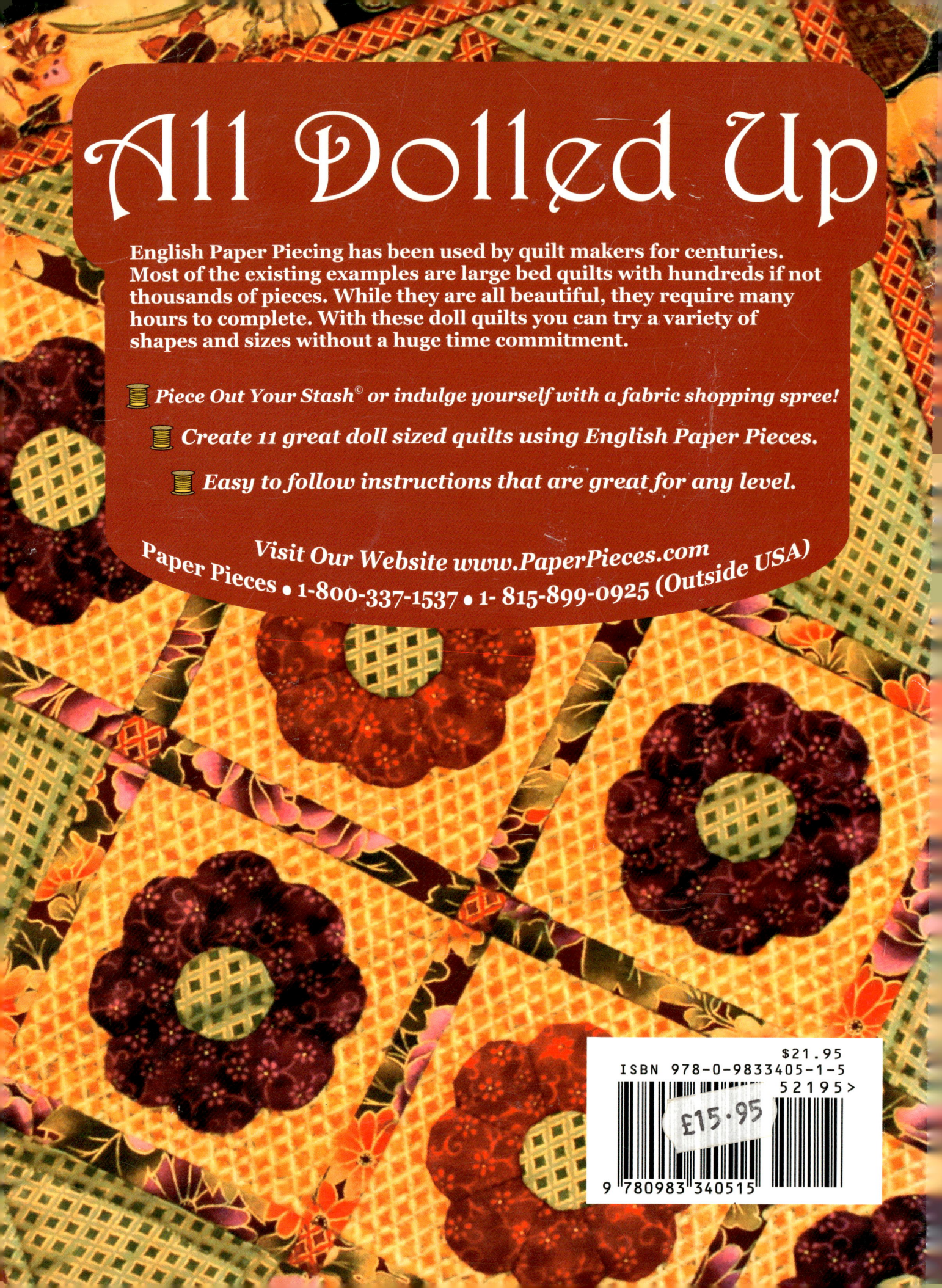

English Paper Piecing has been used by quilt makers for centuries. Most of the existing examples are large bed quilts with hundreds if not thousands of pieces. While they are all beautiful, they require many hours to complete. With these doll quilts you can try a variety of shapes and sizes without a huge time commitment.

- *Piece Out Your Stash*© or indulge yourself with a fabric shopping spree!
- Create 11 great doll sized quilts using English Paper Pieces.
- Easy to follow instructions that are great for any level.

Visit Our Website www.PaperPieces.com

Paper Pieces • 1-800-337-1537 • 1- 815-899-0925 (Outside USA)

$21.95
ISBN 978-0-9833405-1-5
£15.95